Total Recall

Dedicated to my grandparents, Judy and Dennis, and to Philomena Little, my first tutor. They all set me on the right path.

Total Recall

How direct democracy can improve Britain

Nick Cowen

Civitas: Institute for the Study of Civil Society
London
Registered Charity No. 1085494

First Published December 2008

© Civitas 2008
77 Great Peter Street
London SW1P 2EZ
Civitas is a registered charity (no. 1085494)
and a company limited by guarantee, registered in
England and Wales (no. 04023541)

email: books@civitas.org.uk

ISBN 978-1-906837-01-3

Independence: Civitas: Institute for the Study of Civil Society is a registered educational charity (No. 1085494) and a company limited by guarantee (No. 04023541). Civitas is financed from a variety of private sources to avoid over-reliance on any single or small group of donors.

All publications are independently refereed. All the Institute's publications seek to further its objective of promoting the advancement of learning. The views expressed are those of the authors, not of the Institute.

Typeset by
Civitas

Printed in Great Britain by
Hartington Litho Ltd
Lancing, Sussex

I know of no safe repository of the ultimate power of society but the people.

Thomas Jefferson

Contents

Author

Nick Cowen is a philosophy graduate from University College London and an honorary research fellow at Civitas. He has previously written *Swedish Lessons: How schools with more freedom can deliver better education* (2008) and co-authored a number of Civitas reports including *Ready to Read?*. He is also a volunteer teacher for the Language of Liberty Institute.

Acknowledgements

Thanks are due to John Matsusaka and the Initiative and Referendum Institute at the University of Southern California; to David Conway and Anastasia de Waal for their comments on drafts of this report; and especially to Bettina for putting up with me while it was completed.

Executive Summary

- **Direct democracy is a broad term identified here with four key features:**
    - **Citizen legislators**
    - **Localism**
    - **Democratic controls on officials**
    - **Citizen justice**

- Though sometimes presented as radically opposed to representative democracy, direct democratic mechanisms can perform admirably as a check and additional control within a system of representative government. This is true both in Switzerland and the United States

- **Direct democracy has both prevalence and success in the United States though at the state rather than federal level:**

- *Citizen legislators*:
    - 49 states require referendums when amending state constitutions
    - 18 states allow citizens to initiate ballots on new constitutional amendments through a petition
    - 23 states allow their government to refer measures to a referendum

- 24 states allow their citizens to force a referendum on decisions taken by their legislature through a petition

- 21 states allow their citizens to initiate new legislative measures and have them placed on a referendum ballot

  (Petition-size requirements vary from three to 15 per cent of the electorate)

- *Localism:*
  - 48 states provide some form of 'home rule' powers to local districts, allowing structural, functional and fiscal decisions to be taken by local communities

- *Controls on officials:*
  - 18 states allow elected officials to be recalled from their posts by a petition of between 12 and 40 per cent of voters, forcing special elections for their offices

  - 21 states have term-limits for representative legislators, 37 for executive officers such as governor

  - The 22nd amendment to the US constitution requires the president to stand down after two terms

- *Citizen justice:*

  - 22 states require the use of grand juries to indict (prosecute) individuals for suspected crimes.

  - The 5th amendment to the US constitution requires the federal government to use a grand jury to indict individuals for serious suspected crimes

  - Grand juries are also used to investigate the conduct of public officials

- **What is wrong with parliamentary democracy in the UK?**

  - Parliament nearly delegated a huge raft of its own powers to ministers and other agencies under the infamous 2006 'Abolition of Parliament Bill'

  - Parliament continues to delegate many legislative powers to agencies that are not held properly accountable to the electorate

  - Further integration into the EU, the most powerful agency with delegated legislative powers, represents a significant constitutional shift that the British people have no statutory power to control

  - MPs appear to have become immune to prosecution for certain crimes that were created to prevent them from receiving secret donations, and are generally not held to accountable for their conduct

- **How to improve democracy in the UK:**
  - Allow citizens a right of referendum on constitutional issues
  - Allow citizens to challenge any law passed by parliament by forcing a referendum using a petition of five per cent of the number of votes in the last election
  - Allow citizens to initiate new legislation and put it to a vote in a referendum using a petition
  - Give local communities the opportunity to create their own local charters through local initiative and referendum powers
  - Allow constituents to recall their MP from parliament and hold a by-election using a petition of 20 per cent of local electorate
  - Re-introduce a grand jury system to investigate and begin prosecutions of public officials
  - Permit grand juries to be convened to decide on public prosecutions as an alternative to the Crown Prosecution Service

1

What is Direct Democracy?

*Our constitution does not copy the laws of neighbouring states;
we are rather a pattern to others than imitators ourselves. Its
administration favours the many instead of the few; this is why
it is called a democracy.*

Pericles[1]

The concept of direct democracy has been associated
with a broad range of political ideas, but the unifying
theme centres on the definition of democracy itself:
rule of the people by the people for the people—as
opposed to rule by a foreign power or by a ruling class.
'Direct' is often treated as a synonym for 'pure', when
direct democracy is compared with representative
government, where, rather than having rulers held in
check by occasional elections, the distinction between
rulers and ruled has been broken down so as to be
identical. The mere election of rulers by the ruled is
rejected in favour of every citizen being a ruler in their
own right.

But how is this democratic ideal interpreted? The
city-state of Athens where democracy was introduced
in 590 BCE provides an original set of institutions by
which to judge other systems. Democracy in Athens
centred on a single assembly, which all citizens over 20
could attend and vote in. The assembly enjoyed
complete legislative supremacy, unbound by any
written constitutional law or executive authority. An

additional administrative body consisted of 500 citizens aged over 30, who were chosen by lot and served for one year only (apart from military generals). Due to the rapid turnover of officials, it has been estimated that around a third of Athenian citizens could expect to serve on the executive council during their lifetimes. A third pillar was a powerful judicial system which also drew its legitimacy from the citizenry rather than a particular class or expertise. Large juries were selected by lot from citizens who volunteered. They could call anyone for trial to answer charges, including public and military officials.[2]

Hence, with reference to ancient Athens as an initial model, the concept of direct democracy includes the following key features:

1. Citizen legislators. The highest power in the city-state of Athens was an assembly that all citizens could attend, limited by no ruler or written constitution.

This is the strongest and most visible connotation of direct democracy: the participation of citizens in making laws. Within city-states, or at the local level, an assembly (or 'town hall meeting') can allow any citizen to address every other citizen before a free vote on the issue. However, on any scale larger than permits everyone to vote at a single meeting, the vote has to be managed via ballot mechanisms. These can be divided into the **referendum** where citizens are asked to approve (or veto) a measure put forward by a representative assembly, and the **initiative** where voters are asked to vote on a measure that has been put on the ballot by a petition of citizens.

2. Localism. The number of citizens in the city-state of Athens numbered in the tens of thousands, comparable to the approximately 63,500 electors in each MP's parliamentary constituency in the UK.[3] This principle can be applied in nation states through the use of **federalism**, and **localism,** which allows local districts within states a wide range of powers to govern their own affairs.

3. Controls on officials. Most political officials in Athens were selected by lot rather than standing for election. Even officials whose positions were judged to require special expertise (such as those in the military) were subject to democratic oversight and could be removed by the assembly. Athenian citizens also faced the prospect of **ostracism**: exile from the city ordered by a majority vote. Such votes were frequently directed at those who were thought to abuse positions of political power.

In modern states, government officials tend to be elected or appointed on the basis of their expertise rather than random selection. However, the principle of consistent democratic oversight can be re-introduced through the use of the **recall** mechanism. Like an initiative (but directed at an official rather than a legislative measure), recalls allow a petition of citizens to trigger a referendum on whether an elected official remains in place or is replaced by someone else. This allows officials who are suspected of corruption or incompetence to be removed from office before the end of their appointed term. **Term-limits**, which prevent incumbent politicians from standing for the same position repeatedly, are another mechanism for preventing a select few individuals from developing a permanent power-base within a government.

4. Citizen justice. In Athens, there was no public prosecutor and plaintiffs were called to court by a group of citizens. A large powerful jury of randomly selected citizens judged each case against individuals and officials, making the judicial system a powerful, if unpredictable, control on the rest of the government. The jury also decided on the punishment if the defendant was convicted. As a consequence, there was very little reliance on professional lawyers and citizens decided whom to indict, when to convict and how to punish.

While modern legal systems involve many more professionals at every stage, there are equivalent mechanisms for introducing citizen involvement, especially in legal systems in the English tradition. Besides a right to **trial by jury**, **grand juries** can be used to allow citizens to decide when to charge individuals with an offence, balancing out the powers of a public prosecutor, and can act as a further control on public officials.

Of course, the government of ancient Athens would not be considered a functioning democracy by today's standards. Women had no political rights and citizens were permitted to keep slaves. During trials, there were no rules to prevent juries from heckling or shouting down speakers and, with no rules on the admissibility of evidence or rumour, a fair trial was far from guaranteed.[4] For these reasons, ancient Athens would have more in common with South Africa under apartheid or the United States before the abolition of slavery in terms of institutional attitudes to equality before the law and human rights than a modern Western democracy.

With this in mind, operating a set of voting mechanisms along democratic lines (whether direct or representative) might only imply the emancipation of a segment of the whole population under a government's jurisdiction. Democracy, in the sense it is generally understood, means rather more than that and its success as a just institution depends on the underlying relationship between the state, civil society and the individual. What use is a jury trial to women in a society that does not respect their equality before the law? What use are free elections to a political activist if their rights are not extended to freedom of speech and the press, and they face the prospect of being detained for holding their views? Indeed even the right to vote and take part in political discourse is not necessarily associated with other rights. For example, the Labour government has set out legislation to raise the compulsory age of education to 18 years,[5] and adopted a policy of lowering the voting age to 16.[6] If these policies were enacted at the same time, people from the age of 16-18 would have the right to vote but not the right to work. These issues, of the nature of government power with respect to individual rights, are prior to the discussion of which voting mechanisms produce more effective government. Yet the conception of these rights will depend on the character of the democracy that the society believes in.

This character of democracy can be considered in two more or less distinct ways. The first, which we might call communitarian (though it comes under many other labels), is the belief that a pure democracy is the rule of everyone by everyone else, when sovereignty is pooled into a state in which everyone has a vote but no-one has a veto. In other words, a great majority of decisions about society and its objectives will be taken collectively, subject to public deliberation, with a vote either at an assembly or at the ballot box. Rights and liberties might very well be afforded to individuals in a community, but their legitimacy will be drawn from the democratic mandate of the people as a whole.

The second characterisation, which we might call libertarian, holds that individuals possess certain rights prior to whatever any community or state affords them. The ideal democracy becomes not so much everyone ruling everyone else, but self-government, of each individual ruling himself or herself. Individual rights become the foundation of any democratic government, of which the primary purpose is to protect the life and liberties of individuals rather than to set an agenda for what the community or society as a whole will do. Such a settlement will impose strict limits on government, and the main question when considering the success of democratic institutions is what checks and balances will prevent a government from infringing the rights of individuals.

Direct democracy, at least in theoretical discussion, has been associated more with the former communitarian characterisation than with the latter. Rousseau, frequently cited as an early exponent of direct democracy, believed that sovereignty invested in a state was not the property of individuals but a 'general will' that a well-functioning state properly followed. He saw representative democracy as inherently inconsistent with this general will: 'Sovereignty cannot be represented… It consists essentially of the general will, and will cannot be represented.'[7] As a consequence, Rousseau, in the words of Sir Ernest Barker, became 'the votary of the contemporary Swiss canton and the apostle of the ancient civic republics of Athens and Sparta'[8] where government centres on a single assembly, 'with no representatives, without any parties, and within the confines of the small State'.[9] By taking this stance, Rousseau rejected as a sham the sort of liberty offered by English parliamentary democracy, which he believed to be feudal in essence:

> The English… are free only when they are electing members of parliament. Once the election has been completed, they revert to a condition of slavery: they are nothing. Making such use of it in the few short moments of their freedom, they deserve to lose it.[10]

This highly oppositional stance seems to imply that direct democracy is incompatible both with representative democracy and the libertarian characterisation of democratic rights. Yet this theory is at odds with how direct democracy has been seen to operate in practice, often benefiting representative institutions and institutional protections of individual liberty alike. Switzerland, Rousseau's home, has a flourishing representative government and is also a leading nation in terms of respecting individual rights.[11] This does not stop it being a world leader in direct democracy, displaying many of the key features discussed above. Switzerland has a systematic procedure of referendums and initiatives at the national level. Amendments to Switzerland's restrictive constitution must be majority-approved in a referendum. A petition of one per cent of qualified voters is sufficient to challenge any piece of parliamentary legislation, forcing it onto a referendum ballot. Two per cent is sufficient to initiate a referendum ballot on any citizen-directed piece of legislation regardless of parliamentary wishes, giving groups of ordinary citizens near parity with the representative legislature.

In addition, Switzerland is not a large country, having a population more comparable to London than England. Yet it is also a federal state, with most decision-making devolved to 26 cantons. These are themselves composed of around 3,000 communities. Each canton and community has its own set of referendum and initiative procedures and some of the smaller districts continue to allow citizens to express their will in an open 'Athenian style' assembly rather than at the ballot box.

An essay by Brian Beedham in the June 2006 edition of *Civitas Review* provides a useful and detailed explanation of the Swiss system.[12] However, this report focuses on direct democracy in the United States and what Britain can learn from it. The US shares many similarities with Britain's institutions and outlook, and thus offers some extra lessons for the United Kingdom. It illustrates how direct democracy can operate within a large nation-state and be introduced into a constitutional framework that did not originally make significant space for it. Indeed it is arguably a good example of a country where direct democracy plays a more antagonistic role in reforming other institutions than in Switzerland — a role it would probably play at least initially if it became a greater feature of British government.

The various branches of the US government were designed from the outset to be limited, with a heavy burden of checks and balances. In this context, the benefits of direct democracy in the US are a matter of some controversy. While aspects of the model above have been part of the American system from its foundation, many of them are more recent additions that had to be hard fought for by reformers, who were dissatisfied by the institutions of government that were originally put in place. They have come under the banner of anti-federalists, populists, progressives and communitarians whose views have frequently opposed the US settlement as a constitutional republic with a limited representative government. Indeed, the legislative aspects of direct democracy under some stricter interpretations of the US Constitution, which guarantees the people a republican form of government at the state level, would be illegal.[13]

Consequentially, the use of direct democracy varies tremendously from state to state in the US and is arguably at odds with many of the representative institutions that exist alongside it. However, it is this tension between representative and direct democracy in the US that has more lessons for the UK, which has a similarly strong tradition of representative government. While the Swiss tend to consider direct democracy to be a common form of legislating, Americans in general consider it supplementary to the representative legislative process. It is often described as 'the gun behind the door', a reserve power that citizens use to challenge the decisions of their representative legislators when they threaten the rights and interests of the general public. Hence, though not always conceived in this way by the reformers who championed it, direct democracy has arguably been integrated into the US system as an additional check on government.

The first chapter of this report provides an overview of the historical development of direct democracy in the US. The second describes the mechanisms of direct democracy and their prevalence. The third chapter turns to Britain, describing some current problems facing our representative government. The fourth describes how to introduce some additional citizen powers based on direct democracy to remedy the situation.

2

The American Way

As the people are the only legitimate fountain of power, and it is from them that the constitutional charter, under which the several branches of government hold their power, is derived, it seems strictly consonant to the republican theory to recur to the same original authority... whenever it may be necessary to enlarge, diminish, or new-model the powers of government.

James Madison, Federalist No. 49

The addition of direct democratic mechanisms to the US is perhaps best described in terms of three broad phases: the founding of the United States, the populist movement starting in the 1880s, and the conservative revival of the 1970s. In each era, proponents of direct democracy have been allied to various different ideologies, making it a tool that cannot be said to favour either the Left or the Right side of the political spectrum.

First principles

Each US state was founded with the ratification of a constitutional document setting out explicitly the relationship between the people of the state and its government. Although all states established a representative government to legislate, the fact that all state constitutions drew legitimacy from the right of free people set the precedent for referendums as a method of legitimising the creation of a state government. This happened explicitly in the case Massachusetts, which became the first state to hold a statewide referendum to adopt its constitution in 1778.[1] It was rejected, forcing it to be rewritten in terms that the voters found acceptable in 1780. This was followed by a successful referendum on New Hampshire's constitution in 1792, although it was not until 1857 that the US Congress passed a law requiring all future state constitutions to be ratified by the voters in a referendum.[2] This helped to establish state constitutions (though not the US constitution itself) as founded upon democratic mandate that institutes limits on representative government.

Today, 49 states require any amendments to their constitution, proposed by their legislature, to be approved by voters in a referendum before passing into law. The one exception is Delaware, the second smallest state in the union.[3] This is the most widely accepted right to direct democracy, allowing voters a referendum whenever the state legislature proposes a change in the relationship between state government and its citizens, or wishes to introduce laws that will bind future legislatures. It is significant to note that the highest law at the state level can only be changed in the vast majority of states with a direct and explicit mandate from the people in the form of a ballot referendum. This is the case whoever proposes the initial amendment, and regardless of the number of representative legislators in favour of the change.

This is not to say that state constitutions are set in stone. They are living legal documents, frequently being revised. The median number of amendments in each state per year is one, although there is significant variation on this front. Vermont, on average, amends its constitution only once every four years while Alabama has over seven amendments each year on average (although many of these amendments apply only to specific Alabama counties).[4]

A first attempt at providing an initiative on constitutional amendments, in other words allowing citizens not only to ratify but to propose changes, also goes back to the founding of the US. The 1776 Georgia constitution had a provision that was designed to allow a petition of a majority of voters in each county to call for a convention to amend their state constitution. But this procedure was never successfully put into practice.

How the West was won

It was not until the 1890s that initiatives were successfully introduced to the United States as part of the growth of the populist and then the progressive political movements. The causes of these political movements are complex but, in essence, relate to demographic changes brought on by the United States's transformation from an agrarian to an industrialised economy. This changed the balance of power in such a way that new business interests (frequently railroad companies) were able to accumulate wealth and generate political influence disproportionate to the previously dominant agricultural interests. Farmers suffered from dramatic falls in food prices due to new techniques of mass production. Political reform was seen as a way of addressing the imbalance created by the 'machine politics' of powerful local political parties funded by business. Caroline Tolbert, a political scientist at Kent State University, Ohio, explains that 'frustration and alienation with government' started with farmers and miners who were the first wave of reformers and mainstay of the populist movement.[5]

The Progressive Party was a second wave made up of a coalition of Populist interests along with 'upper-middle-class professionals'.[6] John Haskell, Senior Fellow at the Government Affairs Institute, summarised the Progressive movement as mostly 'on the left side of the political spectrum, sometimes the far left... pursuing a policy agenda that included stiff regulations on business, redistributive economic policies, and a pro-labor agenda.'[7]

The nature and legacy of these reforms is an area of great controversy. According to Richard Braunstein, associate professor in political science at the University of South Dakota: 'interpretation of political reform during the pre-World War I era range from an explicit democratic promise to put more power in the hands of citizens to a disingenuous manipulation of democratic rhetoric for selfish gain.'[8] Regardless of their motivations, however, Braunstein contends that: 'Transformations in socio-economic conditions created pressures on political structures, which consequently led to the alteration of accepted practices and procedures that were no longer sufficient to meet the new needs growing out of changes in social and economic life.'[9]

Direct democracy was a major plank of this movement, designed to disrupt the relationship between elected representative and special interest groups. Inspired in part by the initiative and referendum mechanisms of the 1848 Swiss Constitution, Populists and Progressives began to push for their adoption via constitutional amendment in US states. South Dakota was the first state to adopt these mechanisms at the state level in 1897, followed by Utah in 1900 and Oregon in 1902.[10] The reforms continued to spread until the entire West coast of the US and much of the Midwest had initiative and referendum procedures. The East coast proved more able to resist the call of direct democracy, although not for want of activists trying. Local political systems on the East coast were, in general, more entrenched but also somewhat less corrupt than those further West, with only Massachusetts (1918) succumbing to the initiative and referendum processes for all forms of legislation, with Maine in 1908 and Maryland in 1915 adopting more limited versions of the process.[11]

It was the two decades running from 1897 to 1918 that saw the growth in provisions in these mechanisms, with 22 states adopting some form of initiative and referendum. Using these mechanisms, Progressives enacted many laws relating to labour and business practices, including 'the eight-hour workday for women, child labor laws, mother's pensions… and environmental legislation'.[12] The initiative and referendum, however, were arguably just the beginning of the Progressives' political reform agenda. As Tolbert explains:

> While the Progressives are commonly remembered for lobbying for the passage of direct democracy provisions (initiative, referendum and recall) at the state level, what is less well understood is that once these mechanisms were in place, the Progressives relied on the initiative process to adopt much of their reform agenda. The Progressives most important innovation may have been to use the initiative process as a catalyst for political reform.[13]

Many of these reforms are now considered essential to a fair and functioning representative democracy. For example, initiative ballots were used to promote the cause of women's suffrage and successfully implement it directly in the states of Arizona, the state's first ever initiative, and Oregon in 1912,[14] seven years before the right of women to vote was enforced nationally by the nineteenth amendment to the constitution.

It was also Progressive initiatives that radically altered how people were elected to the United States senate, the closest equivalent to the United Kingdom's House of Lords. Before 1913, senators could be chosen not by the people in state elections but by the state legislature. In 1908, Oregon voters successfully introduced an initiative, which instructed the legislature to select the 'people's choice' for US senator. The law (known as the 'Oregon model') was imitated rapidly by the states of Arizona, Arkansas and North Dakota before being made a federal law in the form of the seventeenth amendment to the United States constitution.[15] This instructed all states to elect its two senators by a vote of the people as is still the case today.

Some reforms had implications for other aspects of direct democracy. The ability of the people to recall state officials had become a feature of the Populist movement and became a platform of both the Populist and Socialist Labor parties during the 1890s. The introduction of the recall started within local communities, and in 1903, the city of Los Angeles.[16] Its extension to state level offices followed closely behind the initiative and referendum reforms, also tending to take root in the Midwest and on the West Coast. Oregon adopted provisions for the recall for elected officials in 1908, followed by California in 1911. Arizona, Colorado, Nevada and Washington all adopted the recall in 1912, though Washington did not include elected judges as eligible for recall.[17] 'Home Rule' (see below), where more powers were delegated from the state level to local municipal or county governments, was also heavily promoted by Progressives. For example, 'home rule' provisions were successfully implemented by initiative in Colorado in 1912.

The new Progressives?

This expansion of direct democratic procedures until 1918 ceased until the second half of the twentieth century, which saw five more states introduce the mechanisms: Alaska in 1959, Wyoming in 1968, Illinois in 1970, Florida in 1972, Mississippi in 1992.[18] As a consequence of the growth of provisions for these processes, it is now more common than not for American citizens to have access to a set of ballot mechanisms. John Matsusaka, director of the Initiative and Referendum Institute at the University of Southern California, estimates that around 75 per cent of American citizens have access to initiative and referendum procedures at either the state or local level. The distribution of initiative powers reflects the expansion at the state level: in a sample of cities for one study, Matsusaka found 'initiatives are most likely to be available in the West (95.8 per cent cities) and least likely to be available in the Midwest (63.6 per cent) and Northeast (65.4 per cent).'[19]

The actual use of initiatives to introduce citizen-led legislation first waxed and then waned from the 1900s up until the 1960s, in line with growth in the introduction of the mechanisms. Growing from 23 statewide initiatives in the whole of the US between 1900 and 1910, it reached a sudden high point between 1910 and 1920 with 274 initiative ballots, but failed to reach that level again for the next 50 years. In the 1960s, only 98 initiatives had been placed on ballots nationally and the trend appeared to be one of decline of interest in the mechanism.[20]

This trend shifted with the launch of the modern initiative movement of the 1970s. In contrast to the pre-war Progressive movement, and reacting to a very different political establishment, this movement was mostly conservative in nature, with a focus on controlling government spending. California's Proposition 13 became iconic of this era, described by

Stephen Moore in 1998 at the Cato Institute, as 'a political earthquake whose jolt was felt not just in Sacramento but all across the nation',[21] and is sometimes considered a harbinger of the tax-cutting Ronald Reagan presidency. Officially titled the People's Initiative to Limit Property Taxation, 'Prop 13' initiated a state constitutional amendment passed in 1978 that set a cap on property tax, as well as introducing more stringent legislative requirements for raising other sorts of taxes. Since then, initiative use has been on an upward trend, going from 177 on a state ballot in the 1970s, to 247 in the 1980s and 379 in the 1990s. From 2000 to 2006, there were 301 initiatives and, coinciding with the 2008 presidential election, there were 59 more initiatives, putting this decade on course to at least match the 1990s.[22] In contrast to its Progressive roots, Haskell describes direct democracy today as encompassing 'a wide range of causes left to right, from animal rights to ending racial preferences'. However, 'most of the energy is on the right… exemplified best by the term-limits advocates and the tax rebels'.[23]

Although the political background of those making the greatest use of direct democracy has changed since their introduction by the Progressive movement, arguably the people petitioning for initiatives today have more in common with their forbears than some might imagine. They oppose what they see as special interests embedded within the representative political system and have more success at appealing directly to voters than to the dominant parties within the political establishment itself, in order to introduce limits on government officials. The only difference is that while the original Progressives introduced constraints on representative government through promoting more democratic mechanisms, this new wave of activists tends to use those very same mechanisms to introduce constitutional and statutory limitations on government in general. John Matsusaka accounts for the changing character of the activists by finding that the processes tend to balance out against the current positions of a representative government: 'The initiative is best seen as a device to push policy back toward the middle of the political spectrum when the elected government strays too far in the conservative or liberal direction.'[24]

Taxation

Tax reform has remained an enduring component of direct democratic politics. Bill Piper, examining the period of 1978 to 2000, found that 131 tax initiatives were placed on statewide ballots, more than 15 per cent of all initiatives over that period. The picture painted by these initiatives, as well as their approval or rejection at the ballot box, is neither anti- or pro-tax but highly instructive as to what sorts of tax reform attract majority support.[25]

Sixty-one per cent of initiated tax measures were defeated, a higher failure rate than the average initiative. Initiatives that reduced the tax burden were somewhat more likely to be passed than those that amounted to tax increases but they were still more likely than not to be defeated: 47 per cent of proposed tax cuts were passed compared with 37 per cent of tax increases. Their popularity is also highly dependent on political context, specifically what legislatures are offering in terms of tax reform. As Piper explains:

> In both the early '80s and the late '90s circumstances arose that led voters to approve anti-tax measures. These circumstances (namely increasingly burdensome taxes and reluctance or inability of legislators to address the issue) have caused voters to take power into their own hands... When legislators address the tax issue... we see a notable drop-off in the approval rate of anti-tax measures.[26]

Of the 12 initiatives that were simple tax cuts, five were passed, while the 12 that introduced general rules limiting taxation were more popular, with seven passing. Three initiatives that indexed tax rates against inflation all successfully passed in California, Montana and Maine. Rather than reducing or increasing tax as such, these measures simply ensured that citizens could not be moved into a higher income tax bracket by a rise in inflation.

From this, Piper suggests that, rather than tax cuts as such, 'the most important fiscal policy that voters seek is stability—stability in tax rates, stability in the level of tax increases, stability in the overall tax structure'.[27] In this respect, it seems that direct democracy has operated both as a safety valve when an electorate suffers from instability under a particular tax structure, but also as a useful signal for representatives, prompting them to offer prudent tax controls themselves. Fears that citizens make tax cuts with one initiative, but increase public spending in another, have so far appeared unfounded. Matsusaka: 'there is no evidence that voters irrationally use the initiative to cut their taxes while at the same time increasing spending'.[28]

Public spending

Initiative tax limits have been the major vehicle by which citizens have controlled what state governments have had to spend. There is also evidence that local initiative and referendum powers, a common feature of home rule cities, are a successful control on public spending. John Matsusaka examined the employment policies for public sector workers in 500 cities, comparing those with and without local initiative and referendum powers. With attempts to control for other factors, his findings suggest that in general the presence and use of initiative and referendum powers produced a more cost effective public sector. In cities where public sectors workers were permitted to use collective bargaining techniques (through trade unions), wages tended be 5.7 per cent lower with the initiative, while cities with the initiative that had no collective bargaining tended to have 42.62 fewer employees per 10,000 residents than those without:

> When collective bargaining is unavailable, the initiative mainly cuts employment, consistent with a model in which elected officials tend to pad the public payroll with patronage workers. When collective bargaining is available, the initiative mainly cuts wages, consistent with a model in which voters use the initiative to undo supra-market wages that emerge from collective bargaining. The initiative is also associated with smaller employment cuts when collective

bargaining is available than when it is unavailable. This pattern is consistent with the model because higher union wages cause elected officials to cut public sector employment on their own, reducing the need for initiatives to roll back patronage jobs.[29]

This held across the public sector with the exception of administrative workers and the police force. So by 'allowing individuals and groups outside the official government to make policy proposals, breaking the agenda control of elected officials',[30] initiative powers can prevent pay deals or employment policies from reflecting only the interests of employees and public officials. Matsusaka notes that it is not necessarily the use of initiatives that has created this result so much as their availability:

> [A] tax and expenditure limit is one way the employment and wage reductions associated with the initiative can be brought about. However, cuts can also be brought about preemptively by elected officials without the need for an initiative. One possible explanation for the mixed results in the literature is that when voters are interested in implementing employment and spending cuts, they resort to TELs in some cases, but in other cities astute politicians make the cuts themselves in order to prevent a TEL from coming to the ballot.[31]

Minimum wages

The initiative has not only been used to limit government, but also set standards for business. Citizens have used the initiative to increase statutory minimum wages. This type of legislation appears to be increasing in popularity and might be set to become almost an equivalent feature of direct democratic politics for 'liberal' citizens as tax limits are for conservatives. During the whole of the twentieth century, there were seven minimum-wage-law initiatives: four in California and one in Oregon in 1996, and two in Washington in 1988 and 1998.[32] Moreover, in 2006 alone, new minimum wage laws were introduced in six states (Arizona, Colorado, Montana, Missouri, Nevada, and Ohio), this time as part of a coordinated Democratic Party strategy. Echoing the stabilising tax limits above, these initiatives not only increased the minimum wage but also indexed it to inflation so that the level of earnings would remain equivalent to spending power. All six were approved.[33]

Eminent domain

The issue of eminent domain (known as compulsory purchase in the UK) provides a salutary example of how direct democracy can be used to rein in powers that can be abused by representative government, often allied to business interests. It is the power by which states can expropriate property from private owners, so long as they are compensated, and take it into the public ownership or hand it over to other private organisations. This power came under the public spotlight following the Supreme Court case of 'Kelo *v.* New London',[34] which ruled that private land could be redistributed by the state to another private owner for the simple reason of 'economic development' rather than more stringent requirements such as the completion of a public works or the clearing out of condemned buildings. This brought into sharp relief for many US citizens how dangerous this power was in the hands of many state governments, especially when combined with powerful business interests.

Direct democracy has played a central role in challenging this power. In 2006, 11 states put measures on the ballot intending to prevent governments from seizing property in order to transfer it to other private owners. Nine passed while the two that failed (in California and Idaho) included additional provisions requiring state compensation for private landowners if their property values were reduced by new land use regulations.[35]

3

The Mechanisms of
US Direct Democracy

1. Citizen legislators

Initiative constitutional amendments

In addition to virtually all states requiring referendums on amendments by the legislature to state constitutions, 18 states allow amendments to be initiated by the people. This requires a petition of between three and 15 per cent of the electorate (usually either defined by registered voters or votes cast for the last governor), but typically states require between eight and 12 per cent. Nine of these states also require the signatures to have some form of geographical distribution. Florida requires, for example, not only that at least eight per cent of ballots cast in the last presidential election support the petition but also that this include eight per cent each in at least 12 of its 23 Congressional Districts.[1]

Two of the 18 states (Massachusetts and Mississippi) require the amendment proposal to be approved by the legislature before going to a referendum. This is known as the Indirect Initiative Amendment. The remaining 16 states, however, miss out this mechanism and place the proposal directly on the ballot for approval or rejection by the people in a referendum. This procedure, known as Direct Initiative Amendment, allows amendments to be passed without any input from elected representatives, either in drafting or approving.[2]

States also have varying rules for submitting a valid petition. Many place a maximum circulation period for a petition (Massachusetts and Oklahoma limit it to 64 and 90 day respectively) while other states, such as Arkansas, Ohio and Oregon do not have any time limit at all. Deadlines for signature submission also vary from 90 days prior to election (North Dakota, Florida) through a whole year in South Dakota to Montana's more eccentric second Friday of the fourth month prior to election.

Constitutional amendments can be more firmly entrenched than ordinary statutes (particularly in the context of a legislature that is consistently opposed to a particular measure) since the legislature will be unable to remove or change an amendment once they have been passed without holding another referendum. Combined with the fact that state constitutions are not as basically framed as the US constitution, frequently containing law that would be more appropriate as statutes, it is possible for a successfully initiated constitutional amendment to act simply as a more substantial version of an ordinary statute.

Even in states that allow for constitutional initiatives, they are not the common way of amending constitutions. Legislatures usually draft amendments and seek approval from the electorate. For example, constitutional initiatives are most popular in Florida with an average of 0.59 initiatives a year (i.e. more than

one every two years), compared to 2.89 total amendments on average each year (initiated and legislative).
Part of the reason for the popularity of initiative
amendments in Florida compared to other states is that
Florida does not allow initiatives on ordinary statutes.[3]

Legislative referendum

State legislatures are not required by default to put
new laws before the electorate in a referendum before
putting them on the statute books, in contrast with
constitutional amendments. However, 23 states have a
facility that allows the legislature to put particular
statutes on a ballot for approval by the electorate as
propositions. These are often known as 'referred
measures'. Propositions can also be used to ballot for
the removal of statutes. The legislature can also use a
similar mechanism to ballot other propositions (such as
non-binding advisory questions).[4]

Popular or petition referendums

This mechanism gives the electorate a reserve power to
refer enacted legislation to the people before it becomes
law. This requires a proportion of citizens to petition
for a vote to add it to a ballot. Twenty-four states offer
citizens the power to refer a law to the ballot.[5] This
means that the people can cancel a law that has already
been passed by the legislature. Petition requirements
vary significantly between states, from three per cent of
votes cast in the last election for governor in Maryland
to 15 per cent of votes cast in the last general election
for Wyoming. However, typical petition requirements

tend be either five per cent (California and Colorado) or ten per cent (Alaska and Arizona).

Ten states have no restrictions on the sort of legislation that can be challenged by a petition for a referendum, while Kentucky permits referendums *only* on local tax increases. The remaining states exempt some legislation on various other grounds. As a consequence, the framing of the state constitutions can influence how enforceable this power is in practice. Arizona, Colorado, South Dakota and Washington have constitutions that allow legislation to become law unchallenged so long as it is deemed by the legislature too important to delay, financially or otherwise. Colorado's constitution, for example, prohibits popular referendums on legislation 'necessary for the immediate preservation of the public peace, health, or safety, and appropriations for the support and maintenance of the departments of state and state institutions'.[6] In practice, this means that a 'safety clause' can be added to a wide variety of bills, placing them beyond the reach of a popular referendum. Seven other states exempt laws appropriating funds that are needed to continue the support of existing state institutions or programs. Alaska, Montana and New Mexico exempt all appropriation bills and Wyoming excludes both appropriations and dedications of revenue.[7]

Initiative statutes

Twenty-one states allow the people to initiate new legislation. As with initiatives for constitutional amendments, this allows citizens to petition for statutes that have not been proposed by the legislature. Seven of these states put successful petitions before the legislature for approval before going to a public referendum, a mechanism known as Indirect Initiative Statute and often referred to as 'legislature's option'. Sixteen states allow a successfully petitioned initiative to go straight on the ballot (Direct Initiative Statute). Two states, Utah and Washington, employ both Direct and Indirect Initiative Statute mechanisms (with more stringent petition regulations for Direct Initiatives that are permitted to skip the legislatures approval). Although Massachusetts has a primarily indirect initiative mechanism, citizens can force a proposition onto a ballot with a second petition if the statute is not passed by the legislature within a certain time limit.[8]

The size of petition requirement varies from Massachusetts, where 3.5 per cent of votes cast for governor are required, to 15 per cent of votes cast in the last general election in Wyoming. Typical petition requirements tend to fall within five and ten per cent. Some states have stringent geographical distribution requirements such as Nevada, which requires at least ten per cent of votes cast in the last general election in at least 13 of 17 counties. Others, such as Arizona and Washington, have no distribution requirements at all. The circulation period for initiative statute petitions is usually the same as for constitutional amendments and is subject to the same variation across states, ranging from 64 days in Massachusetts to an unlimited period in states such as Oregon and Arkansas.[9]

2. Localism

Federalism and state constitutions

With a population of just over 300 million and covering a territory of just under ten million square kilometres (more than twice the size of the European Union), the United States does not obviously lend itself to strong local government in the way that the Scandinavian countries or Switzerland do. It is also frequently argued by those concerned for individual liberty and self-government within the US that the US Federal government is too large and legislates in areas that the US Constitution does not sanction. For example, public education, an area traditionally reserved to the legislators and government agencies of individual states, has come under increasing national scrutiny to somewhat doubtful benefit.

Nevertheless, the system of federal government does demonstrate a number of structures by which different levels of government can be limited and made more local and effective. The federal government sets out, via legislation, the US constitution and Supreme Court decisions, the relationship that the states of the union have, and the rights that individuals have that state and local governments cannot violate. However, it is the powerful state constitutions that set out, in detail, the relationship between the state and the individual that are a key feature of democracy in the US. State governments can do far more than just implement the policies set by the national government, and rather more than just passing local laws. They can set out how the state's democratic government is constituted, including: its size; whether to have a bicameral or unicameral legislature; what direct democratic mechanisms can augment or limit the legislative system; how much power is delegated to local districts; how the judicial system operates; and whether a particular piece of legislation, ordinance, or executive decision can be legally enforced in a particular state.

This allows local experimentation not just on public policy and law, but also more generally on the size, scope and type of government. With the ability to move freely between these different jurisdictions, US citizens reserve another important right, of exit from a state government that they do not approve of. So while it may be prohibitively difficult for a US citizen to escape the jurisdiction of the federal government, the states laws that each individual citizen is subject to are to some extent chosen. State constitutions also enforce some degree of stability in the type of laws that can be passed. They can be used to hold a particular statute or ordinance to a legal standard, with an independent judiciary making the judgement. This system that sets out a strict hierarchy of laws and judgements is what allows the various checks and balances (including initiatives and referendums) in the US system to operate. This is perhaps best illustrated in practice by the way the controversial issue of gay marriage has been handled using direct democracy, representative governments and state constitutional law. There have been 33 ballot propositions aimed at restricting the definition of marriage to include only heterosexual couples throughout the US, and two separate ones in California. There the first gay marriage ban, known as Proposition 22,[10] was passed in 2000 using an initiative statute procedure: citizens petitioned to put an ordinary law on a referendum ballot and successfully won the subsequent vote. In May 2008, however, the California Supreme Court overturned the statute in a close 4-3 vote on the basis that it violated, according to their majority interpretation, the Equal Protection requirements of the California State Constitution and that the 'the interest in retaining the traditional and well-established definition of marriage' did not warrant an exemption. [11]

Hence, a particular interpretation of the California Constitution permitted its Supreme Court to strike down a law passed directly by the people. This, however, is not the end of the story. In California, judges can interpret constitutional law but the people can also amend the constitution. A constitutional initiative requires a petition of eight per cent of voters. Though a slightly higher hurdle than the five per cent required for ordinary statutes, the signatures were easily attained within a few weeks of the court's judgement. Proposition 8[12] was passed by the same electorate voting on the night of the November 2008 presidential election,[13] banning gay marriage in California in a way that cannot be challenged by any state agency other than another ballot of the people, making their word final in this instance. Whatever one's views on this particular piece of legislation, it shows how judges, legislators and the people have all had input into the passing of new law and how these decisions have all been afforded an unambiguous priority within a legal hierarchy, with the question finally settled (after several challenges and much public discussion) by the will of the people.

Besides these checks and balances operating within states, the nature of having a federation of states, with some fiercely independent Governors and local politicians, means that state governments can, on occasion, act as another check within the national legislative debate. A recent example of this is the ongoing controversy over the rolling out of the 2005 REAL ID act. Similar to the issue of the introduction of ID cards in the UK, the Department of Homeland Security has been eager to introduce a national ID card in the US in the form of a standardised drivers license with new security features. Many citizens oppose this move on the grounds that it represents an additional infringement on civil liberties and privacy and that it is an expensive programme with dubious benefits for security.[14] These views are reflected in many state governments, and many have put up resistance to the scheme of varying strength. 'Rebel states' spearheaded by Brian Schweitzer, the Governor of Montana, have included California, South Carolina, Maine and New Hampshire. They have taken the DHS to the brink by refusing to implement the law and adopting anti-REAL ID motions and laws through their legislatures. The DHS have at least temporarily capitulated by extending the deadline for implementation and, for now, appear to have been put on the back foot despite having federal law on their side.[15]

Home rule

The concept of home rule has almost an equivalent significance to legislative procedures at the local level as constitutions at the state level. Cities, counties and municipalities are given home-rule status when they are granted their own charter, essentially a local constitution. State laws might require local districts to have initiative and referendum procedures as part of their charters or merely have them as options that citizens might choose to adopt. As a consequence, home-rule districts are more likely to have direct democratic mechanisms in place. The vast majority of states have some sort of provision for home rule, with only Nevada and New Hampshire having none at all. The remaining 48 states vary significantly in the scope and depth of provision and, as a consequence, it is difficult to point to a template of how much power home-rule districts have. However there are some broad categories of home-rule powers:[16]

- **Structural**—where local districts are able to incorporate into local governments, write and amend their own charter as well as alter the managing organisation within limits set by the state's legal code. Forty states allow some level of structural control for city municipalities, and 27 states permit county governments similar powers.

- **Functional**—where home-rule powers extend to providing public and social services. Thirty-one states allow functional home rule for cities, 19 states for counties.

- **Fiscal**—where districts are permitted to raise their own taxes to fund services locally. Fifteen states allow fiscal home rule for cities, and around ten for counties as well.

Structural home rule and the ability of citizens to elect and amend their own local charters are perhaps the most innovative aspect of localism in the US. They could be described as a 'localist approach to localism', allowing citizens to decide not just on ordinances but the actual system of making local law. California, once again, marks itself out as a frontrunner with 478 home-rule cities (and permitting any district to become one), along with similar provisions for counties, all with referendum and initiative procedures for charter amendments and city ordinances. On the other end of the spectrum, Wisconsin has very limited provision for home rule under state law, and at the same time only permits advisory referendums at the local county level.

3. Controls on Officials

Recall

As with initiatives and referendums, the recall mechanism does not apply to nationally elected officials, either in congress, the judiciary or the executive. Eighteen states permit the recall of all or most elected state level officials, and some local (county or city) level officials.[17] Around 11 additional states, while not permitting recall of state level officials, do allow the recall of some local officials.[18] It is commonly applicable to officials in home-rule cities. Seven states restrict the use of the recall, requiring petitioners to have grounds for targeting the official.[19] This differs from the legal impeachment procedure to remove someone from office, which requires 'malfeasance' in elected office, since grounds for recall can also include incompetence and negligence. It can also be useful for removing people from office who are suspected of abuse or corruption but where it cannot be proved via a judicial mechanism.

The reasons for initiating a recall, therefore, can be quite subjective and it is on procedural grounds (and getting the necessary level of signatures) where attempts at recall tend to stand or fall. Petitions for recall generally have higher requirements than referendum or initiative petitions: ten of the 18 states require 25 per cent of the electorate, while Louisiana requires 33.3 per cent and Kansas 40 per cent. California has the lowest petition requirement (12 per cent for state-wide offices), but even that is significantly higher than California's referendum petition requirement of five per cent. A recall ballot is a costly procedure as it forces a special election. It is also worth noting that a recall only rescinds a decision already taken by the electorate (to elect an official), rather than putting a new choice before the citizens.[20]

For these reasons, successful recalls are rare compared with the use of initiatives. Only two state governors have ever been recalled: North Dakota Governor Lynn Frazier in 1921 and California Governor Gray Davis in 2003. The latter put the recall mechanism in the public spotlight as the resulting special election allowed Arnold Schwarzenegger to take his place. Cronin estimated that there had been around 40 recent attempts at recalls against state officials in California that failed to reach the ballot.[21]

Term-limits

Besides recalling officials who are incompetent or otherwise unpopular with voters, an additional mechanism for preventing individuals from treating politics as a permanent career pursuit is provided by automatic term-limits, that prevent officials from standing for re-election after a certain number of terms of office. The most famous example of this in the US is at the federal level. The 22nd amendment to the Constitution, passed in 1947, specifies that no one can be elected president more than twice. There have been attempts to introduce term-limits for other offices at the federal level. In 1992, Arkansas introduced an initiative state constitutional amendment to prevent individuals elected in the state from holding more than three terms in the US House of Representatives or more than two terms in the Senate. However, a Supreme Court decision in 1995 (*US Term-limits, Inc v. Thornton*), found that this law violated the Qualifications Clauses of the United States Constitution. As a consequence, it appears that the only way to introduce term-limits on legislators at the federal level would be to adopt a US constitutional amendment, and individual states evidently do not have the option of introducing them for their own representatives.[22]

There has been considerable more success made in recent years at the state and local level, where term-limits are one of the most consistently popular citizen's initiatives. According to Tolbert, 21 states have introduced term-limits for their state officials, although Massachusetts, Nebraska and Washington had their limits invalidated by their own state Supreme Court rulings. Once again, California (along with Oklahoma and Colorado) was responsible for setting the trend by introducing them in 1990. California, along with Michigan, has the strictest term-limits and only allows assembly representatives to sit for three terms (six years) and senators for two terms (eight years). This contrasts with Nevada and Wyoming that have introduced term-limits of up to 12 years for each assembly. In 2000, Nebraska introduced a two-term (eight years) limit for members of its unicameral assembly. These laws passed on overage by a majority of two-thirds in referendum ballots.[23] Thirty-seven states have term-limits for their Governor and other executive offices.[24]

4. Citizen justice

The grand jury

The grand jury is unique in this set of direct democratic mechanisms in that they predate the foundation of the United States itself. Instead of being inspired by the republican revolution, or the Progressive era reforms, the grand jury was an institution that evolved over a number of centuries in England and was exported to its colonies before it was abolished in the first half of the twentieth century. Whereas a trial jury (the sort still familiar in English law), establishes the guilt or innocence of a defendant, the grand jury decides whether it is in the public interest to prosecute; in other words, whether there is a case to answer at all. As Professor Susan Brenner explains:

> Our constitutional framers thought it a sound idea to create structures allowing lay citizens to check government excesses. The jury system, one of the more obvious and enduring of such structures, was included in our governmental framework because of the widespread belief that the community's voice would ensure a more just judicial system.[25]

The radical nature of this protection was demonstrated even before the revolution during the colonial era when a grand jury might be at odds with the interests of the then British-aligned political class:

> In New York in 1735, an attempt was made to indict John Peter Zenger, the editor and proprietor of a newspaper called *The Weekly Journal*, for libel because of the manner in which he held up to scorn the deeds of the royal governor, but the grand jury ignored the bill... When the settlement of America was begun by Englishmen, they brought with them all the civil rights which they enjoyed in their native land, and with them came the grand jury.[26]

The format of the grand jury varies tremendously where it is used but the essence is as follows: up to 24 jurors are selected from eligible citizens in any given jurisdiction. They are presented with evidence and a request to indict (prosecute) individuals for particular crimes. Public prosecutors present the majority of cases but there is nothing, at least traditionally, to prevent any private individual from approaching the grand jury with evidence. The grand jury does not judge the guilt of the defendant, but merely decides whether there is a probable cause for prosecuting, returning either a 'true bill' or 'no true bill' verdict. In this respect, grand juries take a comparable position in the American criminal justice system to one role of the Crown Prosecution Service in the United Kingdom, in that they decide whether to prosecute someone the police or another agency believe has committed a crime.

The content of the hearings and deliberations are secret in order to prevent jurors from being influenced or threatened, and there is no judge to lead the jurors, only a foreperson (and sometimes a deputy foreperson) elected by the jurors themselves. Due to their privileged and ideally independent position, a number of states also use grand juries to investigate the conduct and standards of public officials, and to investigate criminal activity within government. Their main power in this respect is to subpoena (to order the production of) documents and witnesses to testify before them. Traditionally, grand juries have not required the request of a prosecutor to indict an individual. This means it is possible for a prosecutor to approach a jury with one defendant in mind, only for it to throw out that case and indict someone else. Occasionally, jurors have started ignoring the advice of prosecutors entirely and use their subpoena powers to launch their own investigations before indicting a whole raft of people that state officials had not even considered prosecuting. These 'runaway' grand juries are rare in the US today, but have happened in the past to tackle government corruption and organised crime when state officials (sometimes because they have been compromised) have been unable to do so.

The federal grand jury

The right to be prosecuted only after indictment by a grand jury is enforced at the federal level by the 5th Amendment, part of the US bill of rights, that requires a grand jury to charge individuals for all capital and 'infamous' crimes (crimes eligible for a prison sentence of more than one year). Less serious crimes do not require a grand jury indictment but an 'information' filed by the prosecutor to a courthouse. Special federal grand juries are convened to deal with organised crime (which can include government corruption) and are given more time to investigate criminal activity. They do not investigate civil cases. They are made up of between 16 and 23 individuals drawn randomly from the list of registered voters in the district in which the grand jury is convened. They meet as often as prosecutors require them to indict individuals on federal felonies, which means some districts (urban areas especially) might have several federal grand juries meeting simultaneously at any one time, while other areas might only need to call a jury occasionally.[27]

The modern practice of the federal grand jury is a controversial issue in the US. Its theoretical powers to constrain prosecutors can frequently become a guise under which federal prosecutors can launch intrusive investigations. The weakness of the institution is that, without a judge leading the jury, the most experienced legal expert in the room with the jurors is likely to be the public prosecutor seeking an indictment or a subpoena to help them with their investigation. This is more of a problem at the federal level than at the state level as the legal code involved can be much more complicated. Brenner explains that, because of this imbalance, the federal grand jury has gradually ceded power to 'bring charges on its own initiative' without the direction of a public prosecutor, as well as 'its common law power to investigate regulatory matters and to issue reports'.[28] This has not happened through explicit policy; instead knowledge of grand juries' powers under common law has shrunk to the point that they cease to exist in practice. A report from the Cato Institute, a libertarian think-tank, has warned that, 'Under the current federal grand jury system, law enforcement may bypass the constitutional ban on unreasonable seizures and the [5th amendment] ban on compulsory self-incrimination.'[29] Paul Rosenzweig of the Heritage Foundation, a conservative think-tank, explained:

> In too many cases, prosecutors have gone from using federal grand juries for their original purposes—to sift out weak cases and to protect the accused from overaggressive police and prosecutors—to manipulating them by presenting misleading and/or inadmissible evidence and withholding evidence that favors defendants.[30]

Hence, there appears to be a growing consensus among legal theorists that the federal grand jury is in need of reform if it is to retain its original function, to use citizens to check the power of state prosecutors.

State grand juries

State justice systems are not bound by the US constitution to use grand juries to indict defendants before prosecution, but the vast majority of states make some use of them. Twenty-two states require the use of the grand jury for at least some crimes, ten states permit their legislature to abolish the grand jury (nine of which also permit alterations to how the grand jury operates). Seventeen states neither require a grand jury indictment nor explicitly allow the grand jury to be abolished. Pennsylvania permitted its individual courts to abolish grand jury proceedings, all of which did so.[31]

As a consequence of this very broad framework, the extent to which the grand jury institution lives up to being a successful democratic accountability mechanism varies significantly. For example, at the state level there is no statutory guarantee that the grand jury will be randomly selected from all eligible citizens. Instead, some states employ a 'key-man' system, where a jury commissioner is appointed by a district judge and tasked with finding suitable candidates. There are reasonable grounds for this approach, in that random selection of jurors is prohibitively expensive for a court to administrate, and the selected jurors might have more of a grasp of legal principles and be able to function within a meeting. In practice, however, removing the random aspect of grand jury selection can undermine its entire role as an independent check on the criminal justice system.

Larry Karson, a professor at the University of Houston, examined the consequences of the use of this key-man system in one Texas district, and discovered that jurors were more likely to be police officers, attorneys, court officers, probation officers and other people 'propertied', in his terminology, within the criminal justice system.[32] This presents a likely conflict of interest to grand juries considering that police officers are frequently the main witnesses who are brought before them. Selection procedures along these lines mean that the decision over whether to prosecute might be made by colleagues of the prosecution witnesses. Ethnic minorities were less likely to be selected for duty and, in one outstanding case, a significant proportion of one grand jury was composed of members of the same church congregation:

> [A] former district court judge appointed a fellow church congregate as a commissioner. He, in turn, and in full compliance with the Code of Criminal Procedure, nominated four other members of the same church to the grand jury... The doctrines of that one individual fundamentalist church suddenly had the ability to influence the life and death decisions for numerous non-member souls.[33]

Unsurprisingly, it seems that allowing grand jury selection procedures to vary significantly from the random selection used for trial juries risks removing their greatest strength: a check on political and judicial establishments. This issue, and those highlighted by criticisms of the federal grand jury above, would have to be taken into account were the grand jury to be re-introduced to the United Kingdom as an accountability mechanism.

4

Why the United Kingdom Needs Democratic Reform

Whoever introduces new laws, not being thereunto authorized by the fundamental appointment of the society, or subverts the old, disowns and overturns the power by which they were made, and so sets up a new legislative.

John Locke, Second Treatise

I'm against referendums on all subjects. I share the view which 90 per cent of MPs had until 10 years ago that referendums are just a way of getting round parliamentary government and a way of avoiding the House of Commons. I think parliament should be stronger not weaker. Nothing would make parliament weaker than taking major decisions out of its hands and going for direct democracy by an opinion poll.

Ken Clarke MP QC[1]

The British settlement currently concentrates legislative power within the two Houses of Parliament, with significantly more strength held by the House of Commons. A majority in the House of Commons is sufficient to pass any bill into law. With the consent of the House of Lords, the process is much easier. Thus, when one party wins a majority in the House of Commons at a general election (the most likely outcome under the first-past-the-post electoral system), it is permitted to form a government and enact its legislative agenda with few encumbrances for up to five years, until they are required to hold another election. The government does not command the support of the numerical majority of the people, but by winning the majority of seats in the Commons it has the capacity to rule. Neither the government nor parliament is bound by a single legal document as the United States government is.

Nevertheless, this system retains strong representative democratic credentials. Each member of parliament has to be elected by a particular constituency, which should reduce the influence that internal party preferences can have on the individuals who are elected to the Commons. The majority of ministers and secretaries of state are elected MPs as well, meaning that most of the prime minister's cabinet (who exercise the executive powers) have also been directly elected as individuals, even if they owe their appointment to the prime minister. The second largest party form the official opposition in the Commons and are able to interrogate the proposed legislation put before parliament, and propose amendments.

The costs and benefits of this settlement have been hotly contested, along with other electoral issues such as the consequences of Britain's first-past-the-post system of constituency elections. Up until recently, the arguments for direct democracy tended to be based on some level of discontent with this settlement of parliamentary sovereignty. However, there is an alternative argument, which can be drawn from the US experience, that direct democracy offers a necessary check in order to retain this very settlement and strengthen parliament. As shall now be argued,

48

ensuring the continued sovereignty of the British people via direct democratic mechanisms is necessary, not so much to reduce the power of parliament, but in order to save parliamentary democracy from itself.

The problem of a sovereign parliament

Can a sovereign parliament with total legislative supremacy legislate to abolish itself? Rather like the old logical conundrum 'can an omnipotent being create a rock that it cannot lift', it sounds like a diverting hypothetical question of the sort that could amuse scholars. This makes it all the more shocking to realise that two years ago something akin to this conundrum was tested in reality. The answer to the question, as it turns out, is that parliament probably can abolish itself but on this occasion, thanks to several Lords and a few agitating MPs, chose not to.

The Legislative and Regulatory Reform Bill[2] of 2006 was dubbed by democratic campaigners 'the Abolition of Parliament Bill'. Had it gone through without amendments, it would have allowed any government minister to make an order to amend or abolish any Act of Parliament, or secondary legislation, using a statutory instrument. This power was based on an already common procedure where a 'Henry VIII clause' can be added to any bill, which allows it to be amended or abolished by ministers without another Act of Parliament. This new power, however, would do the equivalent of adding a Henry VIII clause to every Act of Parliament, allowing ministers to make new law with radically reduced parliamentary scrutiny and consent.

Rather than having to introduce primary legislation by having three readings in both Houses, full-day debates, line-by-line analysis by committees of MPs and Lords, as well as hearing amendments from members of each house, ministers could reduce oversight of these orders to an affirmative resolution procedure. That is, at most, a short committee debate and an hour and a half debate on the floor of the house. Since the Government also controls debate schedules, not even this minimal level of scrutiny could be guaranteed. No amendments could be tabled in these debates, meaning that these orders could only be approved, denied or withdrawn, removing all the deliberative aspects of the parliamentary process. A Government with a sufficiently strong whip would be able to overcome these minor hurdles much more easily than bringing a new bill before parliament.

Although supposedly introduced as a streamlining of powers already given under the Regulatory Reform Act 2001, in order to simplify existing legislation as part of the government's agenda for reducing the burden of regulation, the scope for amending legislation was far wider than that. The only limitations placed on the powers were:

- The minister making the order had to be satisfied, in remarkably subjective terms, that it was necessary

- Any new crime introduced using this power could not be associated with a penalty of more than two years in prison

- No tax increase or new tax could be introduced

Perversely, however, the bill did not exempt itself from amendment through its own procedures. So had the bill passed as introduced, those minimal safeguards could have been removed later by statutory order, reserving even more powers to ministers in a manner described by David Howarth, Liberal Democrat MP for Cambridge, as 'a manoeuvre akin to a legislative Indian rope trick'.[3] The procedure could even have allowed ministers to amend or abolish the Human Rights Act or Habeas Corpus. In a joint letter to *The Times*, six Cambridge law professors warned: 'we are sleepwalking into a new and sinister world of ministerial power'.[4] They pointed out how the orders issued could be used, giving the example of the abolition of trial by jury, allowing the Home Secretary to place citizens under house arrest and giving the prime minister the power to sack judges.[5]

The Law Society noted how the act would permit legislative powers to spiral from parliament and even beyond ministerial control: 'We are… concerned that the Bill would permit legislative sub-delegation—i.e. an order made under the Act could allow further regulations to be made, but without the safeguards applicable to the making of the initial order'.[6] They criticised the way in which, while safeguards against ministerial overreach were weak but in place, there were no safeguards at all for the use of power delegated to others: 'an Order could allow such regulations, including new criminal offences, to be made by "any person". An Order passed under the new procedure could thus in theory allow delegation of law-making powers to police, shops, doctors, householders, MPs and pressure groups, even the Leader of the Opposition. There appear to be no controls on that person.'[7] Hence, the problem with the legislation was not just the powers it would afford ministers beyond parliament but the additional powers it could allow ministers to legislate to delegate to *anyone*.

As a consequence, the Lords Constitution Committee slammed the bill as well as the process by which it was developed and consulted upon. Lord Holme, Chairman of the Constitution Committee, explained that the Government: 'wanted to give themselves power to change any law with the minimum of parliamentary involvement, thus gold-plating their powers... The simple fact that ministers failed to recognise the profound constitutional importance of the Legislative and Regulatory Reform Bill does not inspire confidence that they would not use delegated powers to introduce constitutional change in the future, without even realising what they are doing.'[8]

Due to the reaction of academics, MPs and activists as well as the Lords Constitution committee, the Government was forced to climb down. It is worth noting, however, that it was not forced to abandon the bill altogether, merely introduce a few more stringent conditions on how these ministerial orders could be used and the level of parliamentary debate permitted (a super-affirmative resolution procedure was introduced which allows Lords and MPs to table amendments as they would in ordinary debates on bills). This raises the possibility that the Government's attempt to expand executive power was simply too brazen and dramatic in this particular case, and that it would still be possible to achieve many of these powers through 'salami' tactics: introducing bills that, by degree, ratchet up the powers of ministers in the future. As Lord Holme commented: 'The way this Bill has been handled shows that with our unwritten constitution simple legislative proposals can drastically affect our law making system and the fundamental relationship between parliament and ministers.'[9]

In this case, parliamentary mechanisms proved sufficient to realise the profound constitutional significance of this bill and to rein it in before it became law. The Government's attitude towards the bill, however, should be of concern to anyone with an interest in maintaining our constitutional settlement. As the Lords committee noted:

> We are concerned by the way in which a bill with constitutional implications has been handled. The consultative process was lamentable: for example, the consultation document on reform of the Regulatory Reform Act 2001 did not capture the full extent of the Government's proposals as they emerged in the original version of the bill. It is unfortunate, too, that the opportunity was not taken to give pre-legislative scrutiny to the bill... the fact that [the Government's concessions] were made during the final stages of the bill's passage through the House of Commons is something of an indictment of the processes of policy-making and legislation.[10]

Jim Murphy MP attempted to calm these concerns by promising not to use the powers the bill afforded to implement what he termed 'highly controversial reforms' and that parliamentary committees considering any orders made under the act would be given proper consideration. The Committee responded:

> Constitutional safeguards cannot depend on ministerial assurances. Although no doubt sincerely made, ministerial pledges may not be regarded as binding by future governments and are liable to be eroded by exceptions. Moreover, such assurances may not be in the mind of future ministers, legislators and officials. The rule of law and the principle of constitutional government require the security of procedures and limitations which are set out expressly on the face of any enactment which empowers ministers to change the statute book by order. The legitimate desire of any Government to deliver change should not be allowed to undermine the need for careful consultation and scrutiny of proposals that may have the effect of altering basic constitutional machinery.[11]

It seems the Government displayed a remarkably blasé attitude to policy making as well as a highly relaxed attitude to constitutional safeguards, preferring to rely on the word of ministers rather than statutory procedures to ensure parliament continued to be consulted on changing primary legislation. The public is frequently derided for lacking enough interest to take part in representative democracy, but we have reached a rather worse juncture when elected officials start to display a similar level of apathy towards the democratic process.

Fog of law

Although the Legislative and Regulatory Reform Bill is perhaps the most egregious example of the Government attempting to legislate to remove powers from parliament and to hand them over to another agency (in this case ministers and secretaries of state), it is only part of a wider trend in legislation that threatens enduring parliamentary sovereignty and, because of that, representative democracy itself. Simply examining the increased volume of secondary legislation, mainly Statutory Instruments, can begin to outline our area of concern.

Using data from the House of Commons library, it emerges that the volume of secondary legislation has increased significantly. In 1950, 2,144 Statutory Instruments were enacted, in 1980, 2,110, but in 2006, 3,509. Cracknell, author of the archive note, comments: 'the number of Statutory Instruments has seen a sharp increase. From around 2,000 a year until the late 1980s to around double that now.' The annual number of pages of Statutory Instruments (a reasonable proxy for their complexity) has also increased, first roughly doubling from 2,970 in 1950 to 6,550 in 1990, then almost doubling again approximately in line with the increased numbers of SIs introduced over the same period, reaching 11,868 pages in 2005.[12]

The powers to make secondary legislation are given usually to Secretaries of State by parent (or enabling) acts passed as primary legislation by parliament. They can allow the appropriate ministers to control particular details of the legislation, including when particular rules come into force and setting the level of fines or penalties for particular offences, or give much wider powers that ministers can exercise within the framework of an act. Many types need some form of approval by parliament (though with much reduced oversight than ordinary acts of parliament). Many types, however, do not and can be enforced at a time of the minister's choosing. They cannot, except under exceptional circumstances, be amended by parliament. This means that the Houses of Parliament are left with a 'take it or leave it' approach to any secondary legislation that is put before them. The Commons, with a compliant government majority, has barely any opportunity to challenge the measures. Oversight of these measures is, as a consequence, very limited.

Even if the powers that secondary legislation conferred on ministers and other agencies themselves were strictly limited, their lack of oversight would still be a cause for concern. After all, the use of parliamentary powers (even borrowed ones) by non-elected bodies or persons implies an inherent lack of accountability. Yet these powers, far from being limited to details, are growing in breadth and often include widespread powers to amend primary legislation. Their distance from elected representatives is extending too. The attempted boundless expansion under the Abolition of Parliament Bill has already been noted, but this was merely the latest in a series of bills that have expanded the powers of ministers to amend primary legislation for the sake of 'better regulation', including the Regulatory Reform Act 2001 (which introduced Regulatory Reform Order type of delegated legislation) and the Deregulation and Contracting Out Act 1994. This trend is set to continue under the draft

Constitutional Renewal Bill.[13] As the Joint Committee on the Bill has noted, it includes a highly ambiguous and extensive delegated power that will allow ministers to make amendments to it:

> One particular issue of parliamentary accountability arises in clause 43 of the Draft Bill which allows the minister by affirmative order to 'make such provision as [he] consider[s] appropriate in consequence of this Act'. Under clause 43(2) that order may 'amend, repeal, or revoke any provision made by or under any Act'.[14]

Once again the delegated power appears to be somewhat ambiguously limited and extends to any Act of Parliament. The Committee has suggested some ways of limiting this power more explicitly. However, even if these proposals are accepted and the Constitutional Renewal Bill is amended, the continued trend is of Government using 'salami tactics' to reduce constraints on the executive slice by slice.

In addition, the Civil Contingencies Act 2004 gives widespread delegated powers (via Orders-in-Council) to ministers in the event of an emergency, permitting them to make a temporary amendment to any act of parliament with the exception of the Human Rights Act 1998. Moreover, the Human Rights Act 1998 itself introduced 'Remedial Orders' which allow ministers to use delegated powers to amend any primary legislation that has been found in court to be incompatible with the European Convention on Human Rights.

All these examples have, to some extent, delegated powers that allow primary legislation to be amended or abolished or added to without full parliamentary scrutiny. Whatever the individual merits, and, in the case of the Human Rights Act particularly, virtuous intentions behind the legislation, the results have been to reduce the power that our primary democratic representative body has to decide to what laws the people of the United Kingdom are subject. These instances, however, pale in comparison to the body with the most widespread enabling powers of them all: the European Union.

The day after tomorrow

The European Communities Act 1972 is the enabling act for the implementation of all EC legislation under our current settlement with the European Union. A significant proportion of EC legislation, regulations, can be made law without any parliamentary oversight at all. So-called 'third pillar' requirements (relating to Justice and Home Affairs) are agreed by inter-governmental decisions and require primary legislation, as do currently any EC treaty amendments. However, directives often need to be implemented as statutory instruments and they make up a substantial proportion of the SIs laid before parliament. In fact, from 1998 to 2005 the number of SIs laid under the European Communities Act ranged from 7.6 per cent to ten per cent of all SIs laid in each session; an average of approximately nine per cent of all SIs.

The significance and sheer amount of EU legislation can hardly be sufficiently emphasised. Lord Triesman, in a response to a parliamentary question, has said: 'We estimate that around half of all UK legislation with an impact on business, charities and the voluntary sector stems from legislation agreed by [EU] ministers in Brussels' and although the purpose of this report is not to discuss the consequences of specific legislation, it is worth noting that Open Europe has estimated that EU legislation was responsible for 77 per cent of the costs of regulation to business from 1998 to 2005.[15] All these are measures introduced via a single (occasionally amended and debated) enabling act. Like other delegated legislation, parliament cannot amend any directive but is required (when it has any role at all) to implement all EU legislation in law.

The powers under the European Communities Act are now set to be widened. This was first attempted through the Constitutional Treaty, but now that has failed in other EU states, it will be achieved through the nearly identical mechanisms set out in the Lisbon Treaty. This has already been implemented in United Kingdom law as the European Union (Amendment) Bill 2007-08. It expands the European Union's remit and institutions on a number of fronts: it introduces an EU president, a foreign minister and diplomatic service, paving the way for a single European foreign policy. Extensive new powers will allow the EU to set common laws concerning criminal and civil legal procedures and asylum law, as well as defining criminal offences and setting minimum sentences. It will allow the European prosecutors to launch criminal investigations, potentially paving the way for a European Public Prosecutor, and give new powers under the Charter of Fundamental Rights to the European

Court of Justice to intervene in UK courts. Further EU 'competencies' extend to more powers over health, social security, employment law, economic planning, public service investment and energy policy.[16] Perhaps most significantly, the treaty now has a self-amending mechanism, allowing a unanimous vote by the European Council to change any text in the part of the treaty that details the Union's functions. This opens up the possibility of almost boundless expansion of European Union 'competencies'. Such changes could potentially be implemented into British law using a mere statutory instrument. As a consequence, this Treaty will represent a step towards further integration into the EU. For the moment, widespread powers to legislate have been delegated from parliament to the EU. After implementation, a mechanism for deciding how widespread those powers are to become, will itself have been, in part, delegated to the EU itself. It facilitates the amendment of enabling legislation, making parliamentary scrutiny one further level removed.

It is worth noting the strange way in which the legislative supremacy of parliament has been used. All the powers exercised, for now at least, are enabled at the behest of parliament passing one piece of primary legislation, the Treaty. Yet, as the Treaty specifies, all secondary legislation passed under the act has supremacy over all primary legislation previously passed by parliament. Hence an inversion is taking place: secondary legislation is becoming superior to and more extensive than the primary legislation that enabled it. Eventually, the more powerful bodies will be those with delegated legislative powers rather than parliament, the primary legislative body. When that stage will be reached is difficult to tell, but as the expansion of EU powers is gradual, this is the emerging trend.

The Treaty referendum

There is no legal requirement for a referendum on the delegation of powers, no matter how extensive, from parliament to other agencies. There is not even a requirement for some form of supermajority in parliament to pass legislation authorising such powers or any act of constitutional significance: a simple majority is acceptable. The Labour government has consistently denied a referendum on the Lisbon Treaty and there is no judicial or ballot procedure to force them to hold one.

As a consequence, arguments for holding a referendum on what has now become the Lisbon Treaty have not, on the whole, been legal arguments. Instead there is the argument from the principle of British sovereignty: essentially that, whatever the legal authority of parliament, it *should* be for the British people alone to decide whether to hand over so many additional powers to a foreign agency. However, it has proved difficult for the Conservative Party in opposition to defend this position when the Conservatives in government were happy to delegate power in the same way to the European Union in 1992 via the Maastricht Treaty—without a referendum. The obvious question that the Conservatives have to answer is: why should the Lisbon Treaty require a referendum if all it does is to expand the powers already given under previous treaties to a few more competencies?

The second argument centres around Labour's 2005 manifesto pledge to hold a referendum on the European Constitutional Treaty. The European Constitution, in that form, was defeated in Dutch and French referendums before the referendum could be placed on a British ballot. However, the Lisbon Treaty is generally accepted to be almost identical to the European Constitution, subtracting one or two symbolic references to the European flag and anthem. It is argued that the pledge to hold a referendum should apply to the Lisbon Treaty, though Labour strenuously deny this, pointing to the so-called opt-outs (of somewhat dubious value) from some of the more controversial elements of the Treaty that they have secured for the UK.

The Lisbon Treaty has not been put to a referendum in France or the Netherlands as was previously attempted and has instead been ratified by their representative assemblies. However, it has now suffered its own rejection by the Irish in their referendum, which they were obliged by their own constitution to hold. In fact, the European constitution has never been ratified by a referendum of the people of any nation, in any form, only ever by their governments. Yet it appears that the rolling out of the constitutional arrangements will continue anyway despite the lack of any direct democratic mandate.

Ireland may have to hold another referendum, since its constitution will not allow it to implement the new European Union institutions without permission from the people, but the people in the rest of Europe will not be directly consulted. This paucity of a democratic mandate for the European Union, now a powerful governing body, is not just a problem for the United Kingdom: it posits a question that is increasingly being asked right in the heart of the EU. The French historian and political philosopher Pierre Manent in a recent interview managed to sum up this ongoing problem of legitimacy in haunting terms that are rarely matched by British commentators:

> The problem in Europe, particularly in France, is that our politics, though obviously bad, are not correctible, whatever the orientation of the electorate. Even though opinion is hostile to the indefinite extension of the European Union, even though the citizens of two founding countries voted against the constitutional treaty, everything proceeds as before and it is being suggested that the treaty will slip in through the window. The European machine has been set up in such a way that it cannot not be deployed, the result being a 'purposeless finality' ('finalité sans fins'). The outcome that we are celebrating, the 25th anniversary of Europe, and soon the 30th, will have been created by a mechanism that no one can control, and that was not desired by anyone.[17]

Whatever the ideals, and doubtless practical benefits, associated with the project for integration into the European Union, the form of organisation it has to offer is no more democratic or localist than the McDonalds franchise. For democrats of all kinds, the EU will remain 'the elephant in the room' with regard to any question of the democratic legitimacy of governing institutions. But what is the alternative? Our system of nearly unfettered representative government seems inclined, when prompted by suitable incentives, to hand its own powers over to the executive, to other agencies and even to foreign agencies. The British can hope that parliament re-asserts itself, but it might be necessary to give it a helping hand, and the tremendous interest in holding a referendum on the Lisbon Treaty points to the solution: direct democracy.

5

Introducing Direct Democracy to the UK

The further the departure from direct and constant control by the citizens, the less has the government the ingredient of republicanism.

Thomas Jefferson

Using our four features of direct democracy, and considering their practice in the United States, we can set out how to introduce more direct democracy to the UK to improve the accountability of representative government.

1. Citizen legislators

The people's veto on constitutional changes

As suggested previously, the right to a people's referendum on constitutional changes is a key feature of direct democracy and the one that would be most useful to import into the UK. How could it be done? In essence, what Britain is missing at the moment is a law or strong precedent for requiring constitutional referendums whenever the government wishes to alter its relationship with the people. This is indicated by the use of referendums so far. They have only a recent, infrequent history in the United Kingdom. At a national level, the referendum has been used only once: in 1975 to decide whether to remain in the then

European Economic Community. There have also been eight regional referendums: in Northern Ireland in 1973 on whether to secede from the UK and join the Republic of Ireland and in 1998 on the Good Friday Agreement; and several on devolving powers (usually in the form of regional assemblies) to Greater London, Scotland, Wales and Northern England.

As a consequence, referendums are rare but growing occurrences at the regional level. National referendums are exceptional but have been discussed in principle by the major political parties more recently: specifically, a commitment to holding a referendum on adopting the Euro as a currency and the promise to hold a referendum on the European Constitution. The Government has also, as part of its reform agenda of increasing the regulation of political parties and campaigning, produced a detailed regulatory framework of the conduct of national and regional referendums. Regulations now specify the timing of the referendum; that the question on the ballot should be reviewed by the Electoral Commission; who may participate in campaigns for or against the question put before the people; and detailed requirements on the financing of such campaigns.

Yet while national referendums have been discussed and legislation has been introduced to regulate them, there has been comparatively little interest in adopting them as a systematic part of our democracy. A key reason is the position that parliament has come to hold within our constitution of legislative supremacy. It is able to pass, amend or rescind any law of the land. It is limited by convention, but is also able to change the procedures by which parliament operates and legislation is passed. The only input that the electorate currently has in national lawmaking is to elect MPs to the House of Commons once every five years (or whenever the current government chooses to call an election).

The form that referendums take, when they happen, reflects the level of control that parliament has over legislative procedure. They are triggered by a government appending a referendum clause to a bill and happen as part of the government's legislative agenda. This has only ever been used, or promised, on constitutional matters so far: the devolution of powers to other bodies like the Welsh and Scottish assemblies and on the UK's settlement with what has become the European Union. However, there is no convention that obliges the government to give the people a referendum, no matter what the substance of the bill. At the same time, there is nothing to stop a government from having a referendum on any bill, whether it concerns crime, finance, health or education. There is no mechanism for the electorate to force a referendum on legislation. Indeed, since no parliament can be bound by decisions taken by previous parliaments, even a decisive referendum against a piece of legislation might legitimately be treated only as advisory, and ignored were a similar bill introduced to parliament without a referendum clause. The trigger of referendums is voluntary, at the behest of the government and parliament; perhaps equivalent to *legislative refer-endums* held in some US states.

The result of this system is that the referendum does not give British citizens any additional powers over the government, but instead creates an additional mech-anism which government may use to their advantage. As Steve Richards, a political commentator, observed at a recent Hansard Society discussion, referendums (or rather the promise of a referendum) can easily become the dustbin of policy. He argued that Tony Blair got round the controversial issues of adopting the Euro and introducing proportional representation for parliamentary elections by simply promising a referendum on each problem, rather than taking the questions head on and deciding whether a Labour government supported them. A government can sit on a policy that it would rather not introduce, and will certainly only ask the electorate for its blessing for a policy it does support if that blessing is relatively assured. As Richards has said, 'a referendum is a device proposed by leaders only when they are certain they can win'.[1] Clearly a referendum will only be held by government in an attempt to cement a controversial policy in place with a democratic mandate. Using a democratic mandate to challenge a government's decisions is currently impossible.

In order to improve this situation, the power to trigger a referendum must be taken out of the hands of government so that they are not the final arbiters of what and when citizens will be consulted on. This is a pre-requisite for allowing citizens to take part in the legislative process. In US states, the almost universally available solution is to reserve the power to approve or veto any state constitutional amendments to the citizens (though not to laws or constitutional amendments passed at the federal level). As the right to a referendum is enshrined in those same state constitutions, it is impossible for governments to take that power away without holding a referendum on that amendment. Undoubtedly, removing the right to a referendum so that legislators could amend constitutions more easily is quite a hard idea to sell to an electorate that is used to retaining this reserve power. This contrasts starkly with constitutional protections in the UK where, as we have seen, bills that change Britain's constitutional arrangements can be passed as simply as any other piece of legislation. Our system of legislation could be described as 'flat', in so far as no type of law has any intrinsic supremacy over any other. Whereas US states permit legislators to introduce any statute that does not break any constitutional limits, in the UK there are no explicit limits.

The first step to introducing limits in the UK would involve altering this 'flat' nature of our legislation. A new and more stringent mechanism for passing bills of constitutional significance would have to be established. Would this necessitate the ratification of a written British constitution with explicit referendum powers? Not necessarily. It might be possible, as the United Kingdom has managed in the past, to develop and retain some form of implicit convention on referendums. This could be based on an underlying understanding that the British people are the sovereign legislature, and that their sovereignty is invested in parliament, giving parliament the power to pass any law that does not divest itself of its own powers or otherwise change this basic relationship between parliament and the people.

Without an explicit constitution, deciding when such a law had been passed would be a difficult question, but there might be an evolved solution under the present system. According to David Pannick QC, 'some judges and constitutional lawyers have suggested that judicial review is now so fundamental a part of our unwritten constitution that there is an implied limitation on the sovereignty of parliament'.[2] If that judicial authority were extended over legislation with constitutional implications, then a judicial decision could become the trigger for a referendum. This would make our unwritten constitution not forever unchanging but always subject to a people's veto.

On the other hand, the current government, through the Constitutional Reform Act 2005, is already introducing one institution inspired by the US system, and this direction of reform may increase interest in eventually adopting a written constitution. The Ministry of Justice is in the process of setting up a United Kingdom Supreme Court, due to come into force in October 2009.[3] One of the drivers behind this institutional change is the desire to remove what has long been considered an anomaly under the present

British settlement. The House of Lords is part of the legislature but also contains the British court of appeals in the form of the House of Lords Judicial Committee. This dual function that its members, the Law Lords, have in both making law and also acting as the court of last resort is arguably a threat to having a fully independent judiciary. Under the new system, justices of the Supreme Court will not also be members of the House of Lords. As the Ministry of Justice claims, the Supreme Court of the United Kingdom 'marks the functional separation of the judiciary from the legislature and the executive'.[4]

So the Government is already in the process of establishing a body that might be a suitable authority to rule independently on constitutional matters as the US Supreme Court does. If an actual constitution were to be finally written down and ratified, it need not contain a significant amount of law itself, and could still allow parliament to keep the vast of majority of its power to legislate. It would set out parliament's obligation to hold a general election, as it does now, every five years. It would also be prudent to introduce some minimal constraints on parliament by enshrining civil rights such as habeas corpus and the right to trial by jury within the constitution. If other judicial constraints on parliament's power to legislate were desired, such as the Human Rights Act, the constitution would be the correct place to enshrine it, ensuring that such constraints were given supremacy over parliamentary bills. Most importantly, the constitution should prohibit parliament from delegating primary

71

legislative powers to any other agency and set out that secondary legislation, whether ordered by ministers or an alternative legislature, cannot supersede an Act of Parliament. Amendments to the constitution itself would require a referendum.

The people's initiative

The value of referendum ballots goes beyond constitutional issues. California has been at the forefront of direct democracy and, although it is the most populous state in the Union with 36 million inhabitants, it has not suffered from conducting frequent plebiscites. On the contrary, it has benefited from some very successful citizen-initiated legislation. With this in mind, extending similar powers to British citizens would certainly be radical but by no means unthinkable or unworkable.

Suppose Britain took this approach to direct democracy and borrowed the Californian model. The main powers that citizens would gain would be to challenge any law passed by parliament with a popular referendum and to propose new laws through petition initiatives. A petition of the equivalent of five per cent of votes cast in the previous general election would be sufficient to place any new piece of legislation on a ballot. Going by the 2005 general election results,[5] that would require a petition size of around 1.4 million people. Citizen initiatives on constitutional matters would require a petition of at least eight per cent of votes cast in the last general election, or around 2.2 million people. An interesting, and useful, consequence of measuring the petition requirement via votes cast would be that the lower the turnout at the last election, the easier it would be for citizens to challenge laws passed in parliament. In this sense, politicians would no longer be competing merely between themselves, but also with active citizens collecting signatures for a petition. If a party won an election but without a large electoral turnout, it would become easier for their decisions in government to be challenged by a petition referendum than it would for a party which had won with a larger turnout, and therefore required a larger petition to challenge them. That would certainly turn the usually abstract concern over whether an election result represents a mandate into a rather more practical concern for politicians who might end up fearing the citizen petitioner more than the official opposition!

The numbers involved in this model are large, but not insurmountable if initiative and referendum legislation garnered enough interest from the elect-orate, and the ways of publicising petition causes are expanding along with communications technology. Indeed, one might say that the infrastructure for large-scale petitions is already in place. Since November 2006, the charity mySociety in conjunction with the prime minister's Downing Street office has established a website allowing internet users to create and sign petitions online.[6] Since then, tens of thousands of petitions and millions of signatures have been submitted as the website has grown in popularity. The petitions have no statutory authority and so do not often challenge or propose a precise piece of legislation, as a citizen's initiative would have to. However, they do offer an indication of the level of interest that petition referendums could attract. Indeed, there has already been one petition, demanding that the government abandon plans to introduce road pricing using surveillance technology, submitted in February 2007, that gained enough signatures (1.8 million) to surpass by some margin the theoretical petition requirement under our British/Californian model.[7] The petition attracted signatures even though it conveyed no statutory duty on the government to alter its course, and has, if anything, only warned the Government to tread a bit more carefully around the issue. If the petition system did have some statutory authority, one can only imagine how much more popular the system would become.

Both the current Labour government and the Conservative opposition have shown interest in joining up the petition system with parliamentary scrutiny of government policy. Harriet Harman, Leader of the House of Commons, has recently set out plans to extend the petition system beyond the Prime Minister's office and allow petitions to be championed by constituency MPs. The Government will be expected to reply to most petitions, while a few will be picked to be debated in parliament or put under scrutiny by select committees.[8] David Cameron, the opposition leader, has gone further, suggesting: 'a system whereby, if enough people sign an online petition in favour of a particular motion, then a debate is held in parliament, followed by a vote—so that the public know what their elected representatives actually think about the issues that matter to them'.[9] It is not clear from this proposal whether the requirement to hold a debate would be statutory, and this is still a far cry from California's citizen-initiated and referred legislation, which can challenge the votes of the legislature. Nevertheless, on a suitably statutory footing, this procedure would become almost equivalent to the indirect initiative mechanism and allow part of the parliamentary agenda to be directed by citizen petitioners.

In its current form, the online petitioning system would be unsuitable for taking a powerful role in the legislative process, such as a trigger for a referendum ballot or placing a bill before parliament. It is vulnerable to people signing multiple times under different identities and there is no way to ensure that only the electorate can take part in petitions. A more stringent system of checks would have to be introduced, but as the success of online banking services demonstrate, it is possible to create a relatively secure identification system and certainly one that is sufficient to prevent widespread fraud: the technology is not an overall limiting factor.

Indeed the main barrier to giving petitions a forceful statutory role, allowing them to launch a referendum on a particular law, is the government. It would remove their monopoly on legislating and force them to share that role with citizen legislators. There is not really a way around this barrier to reform other than to say that, if a political party undertook to introduce a system as described, it would doubtless capture the imagination of much of the electorate and could be a very popular reform that cut across ordinary party boundaries. It also has the potential to re-energise our national democracy, which would benefit politicians as much as the people. A government that managed to secure powers over the legislature to the people would leave a strong democratic legacy for the United Kingdom and permanently alter the balance of power in this country.

2. Localism

Home rule for England
Whereas national referendums and initiatives remain, for now, a somewhat distant possibility, localism is one aspect of direct democracy that commands far more support amongst the major political parties and the current government in Westminster. Indeed, the only risk is that the consensus that local communities and local government are better placed to deliver public services might be more rhetorical than practical. Would it even be possible, in current mainstream political discussion for a politician to propose an explicitly centralising agenda? It is somewhat doubtful. The other problem is that there is enough ambiguity in what localism represents for it to be possible to present almost any complex policy as being part of the agenda. The question, therefore, is not so much about the aspiration to make government more locally account-able, so much as ensuring that any reform actually does so.

The launch of the Communities and Local Government White Paper, *Communities in Control: Real people, real power,*[10] is a case in point. From the over-the-top title, through the ecstatic model citizens in the photographs, to the gushing introduction by Hazel Blears, the presentation is designed to demonstrate how sincerely the government wants to give more power to local and community organisations:

> We want to see stronger local councils, more co-operatives and social enterprises, more people becoming active in their communities as volunteers, advocates, and elected representatives. We want to see public services and public servants in tune with, and accountable to, the people they serve. Democracy is not about a cross in a box every five years, but about a way of life. It should flow around us like oxygen.[11]

Commendable language, but what do these ambitions amount to? In the White Paper, a new duty for local authorities to 'promote democracy' and an extension of a duty to involve local people. In practice, this means introducing a new statutory duty for local authorities to respond to petitions, potentially making them a trigger for an inspection of a local public service by an independent agency, which represents a mere nod in the direction of citizen involvement. The funding strategies remain highly centralised with a raft of ring-fenced grants that local communities will have to prise out of the central government to access. This includes a £70 million 'Communitybuilders' scheme and a 7.5 million Empowerment Fund. Then there is the ironically titled 'Grassroots Grant' fund of £80 million, which is managed by the Office of the Third

Sector, based in Great Smith Street in the heart of Westminster. This avowedly localist set of initiatives seems stubbornly centralist in format.

In addition, the White Paper suggests introducing 'incentives' to vote, including prize draws. As Simon Jenkins explains, this 'gesture localism' does not deal with the root of the problem, the well-founded impression amongst citizens that a vote in a local election is likely to have no impact on local government:

> To make local electors vote, they should be entered for a 'prize draw' to win, say, an iPod or shopping voucher. Instead of the incentive of real power, they should have an incentive of greed. They may not vote because the vote is democratically barren, but they might at least be bribed to do so. [12]

Michael Kenny at IPPR concurs, explaining how this direction does not change the balance of power between Westminster and local government:

> The White Paper does not address two of the major obstacles blocking the path to the rejuvenation of local government and democracy. It does not herald any further transfer of powers in education, health, policing and planning out of Whitehall. Nor does it provide mechanisms for elected politicians or local bodies to exercise meaningful control over these policy areas. [13]

What is the alternative? Direct democratic mechanisms at the local level have already played a role in some of more successful reforms. Since 2001, local authorities have been able to hold a council or petition-triggered referendum on adopting a mayor. Twelve referendums have been successful and IPPR have pointed out some of the success stories:

> In Middlesborough, 'Robocop' Ray Mallon cut crime by 18 per cent in his first year of office. In London, Ken Livingston has pioneered ambitious and agenda-setting policies in relation to transport and the environment, most notably through the congestion charge. In Doncaster, Martin Winter developed a high-profile Fighting Litter, Abandoned Cars and Graffiti (FLAG) campaign. And in Stoke-on-Trent, Mike Wolfe developed a Better Service Fund… which used money raised from an increase in council tax to clean up and improve the physical fabric of the city.

These cases required a significant level of functional and fiscal autonomy, and IPPR suggest replicating these successes elsewhere by encouraging more elected mayors. However, they despair that so few (just three per cent) of local authorities have taken them up under the present procedures for introducing them, laying the blame firmly with the current established local councillors: 'When the idea of elected mayors gained ground in the mid-1990s, the overwhelming majority of councillors were hostile. A poll conducted in 1999 found that only three per cent supported it.' Their methods for breaking up this entrenched group, however, displays an unfortunate centralist impulse. Their two suggestions are:

- A national day of local referendums imposed by central government, with a statutory requirement for all urban local authorities to hold a referendum.

- Abandoning the idea of holding a referendum altogether and introducing elected mayors from the centre, and making them the default form of local government structure in urban areas, keeping the old form of government only when there is obvious popular opposition to an elected mayor.

IPPR embrace this contradiction in their proposals: 'one of the central arguments of this paper... is that, paradoxically, such an act of centralisation is needed to deliver greater local autonomy in the future'. However, while we should be alive to the problems of local political establishments and the barriers they present to change, the temptation to reform by central diktat does not just break the principle of localism but also has its own pitfalls. For example, to some extent the success of elected mayors might be due to their being received by a council and populace that has specifically requested one and that has been prepared (through the grassroots campaign to create the role) for an institutional change. Those councils that had a populace that was engaged and interested in the reform might be the ones that were able, subsequently, to produce suitable candidates for mayors and so make their terms of office a success. That context might be lost when the reform is brought in from the centre for the sake of uniformity amongst urban local authorities. Rather than weighting the rules more in favour of mayors *per se*, a more successful localist strategy might be to allow elected mayors to have more powers in the event of them being adopted, thus increasing the incentive amongst local people to petition for institutional reform. In other words, the best strategy for introducing localist policies is localism itself.

The concept of home rule could act as a solution here. The question is why should local electorates only have a binary choice of governing institutions: 'mayor or no-mayor'. The government certainly extended choice by introducing the right to petition for an elected mayor, but why stop just there? Local home rule powers could take this principle of choice and extend it further by allowing citizens to create, within a broad framework, their own governing institutions and vote to have them enshrined in a local charter. The charter could decide how many local officials are actually needed, whether they should be elected or appointed or selected in some other manner, and whether powers should be reserved to a single elected mayor or to other executive officials. Charters could also introduce other limits on officials, such as term-limits on councillors and recall mechanisms as well as local initiative and referendum powers on bylaws if appropriate. As a consequence, a wider diversity of local government forms could be established to experiment with their respective benefits. So long as some mechanism for citizens to amend or abolish a charter that was not working existed, any mal-functioning set of institutions could be reformed along different lines.

Structural reforms such as these remain of limited benefit while local councils and local public services are statutorily required to follow central government policy and targets. On the other hand, it is perilously difficult to disengage from a centrally managed scheme of regulation without, at least in the short term, jeopardising the standards that a system of government oversight delivers. A home rule approach to local accountability could be used in this respect as well. Rather than trying to get central government to cut down on targets for local authorities and withdraw powers, home rule provisions could allow individual local communities to opt out of elements of government regulation as and when they have a locally decided alternative to replace it.

This still leaves the problem of fiscal independence. The national government does not retain power under the current system merely through statutory means. Another powerful lever of control is the use of ring-fenced funding that can only be unlocked by local authorities if they get involved in initiatives and policies of which the central government approves. This is not an area that can be easily reformed, although the long-term direction of policy would be to split the guidance offered by central government from the funding it provides, such that local government can receive funding without having so many strings attached. Eventually, taxes that are to be spent on local services ought in general to be raised from local communities. In the meantime, home rule provisions could permit (but not require) local councils to vary the levels of council tax, experiment with different sorts of local taxation and to be able to prioritise expenditure in accordance with initiatives chosen by the community.

Devolution

One of the more developed aspects of localism in the UK has been the delegation of powers to its historic national constituents in the form of the democratic assemblies of the Scottish parliament, the National Assembly for Wales and the Northern Ireland Assembly. These devolved institutions remain constitutionally subordinate to parliament and their powers are technically reversible by a parliamentary bill, unlike the federal system of the US.[14] Looking at these institutions from a purely localist perspective is somewhat complicated by the growing strength of a Scottish independence movement, led by the Scottish National Party.[15] As a consequence, this direction towards devolution may eventually turn out to have foreshadowed the break-up of elements of the United Kingdom rather than merely a new settlement towards making the British government more accountable to local citizens. At the same time, the current settlement has a couple of anomalies: MPs in the British parliament elected to Scottish constituencies are able to vote on laws that will not be enforced in Scotland but only in England and Wales, and regional funding arrangements are currently weighted significantly in favour of various regions, especially Scotland.[16]

With that in mind, however, it is possible to see some of the consequences of having devolved administrations that have a family resemblance to some of the checks and balances that the US system of federal government offers more systematically. The Scottish parliament, besides setting local priorities in

public services, has produced a boisterous administration that frequently criticises the government in
Westminster. As an example, in an echo of the case of
REAL ID in the US discussed previously, the Scottish
parliament has been able to take part and influence the
national debate on ID cards in the UK even though it
lacks the statutory powers to prevent the British
parliamentary legislation being implemented.[17] Of
course, for a national government, this might be seen
as a problem, since more assemblies offer more sources
of opposition and criticism when they are not under
the control of the same party, but this is arguably an
example of greater democratic accountability, via
localism, in action.

Devolution has also allowed for greater policy
experimentation and diversity in the delivery of public
services. The issue of conducting national tests in
primary schools offers an example. In education, the
use of 'Sats' exams in English primary schools has
become increasingly contentious as their value as an
assessment measure has been called into question on
many fronts.[18] In response, the Education Select
Committee has produced a report drawing on the
experience of Wales that has abolished these
assessments and introduced more successful alternatives.[19] In this way, devolved regions get to test the
ground for new policies. This strength of devolution is
not being used to its potential. As Nick Pearce of IPPR
explains: 'Whitehall has no process for monitoring
policy innovations from Scotland and Wales, despite
initial claims that devolution would create "policy

laboratories" across the UK'.[20] Nevertheless, the devolved regions are starting to make a hesitant impact on the public policy debate. In this sense, devolution has already been a success.

3. Controls on officials

If we take seriously the need to offer a 'localist approach to localism', where citizens are able to decide how their local governing institutions will be organised within a broad framework, then it would be mistaken to suggest a one-size-fits-all approach to additional democratic controls at the local level. It should suffice to say that controls such as the recall mechanism and term-limits can represent powerful means of preventing politicians becoming complacent or too established in public office.

At the national level, the following controls would represent a significant reform:

A recall for MPs
The idea of introducing a recall mechanism for MPs has gained some interest in light of the recent scandal involving a Conservative MP, Derek Conway, diverting large sums of money from House of Commons research expenses towards members of his family who did little or no work for him. He was removed from the Conservative party but, though he intends to stand down at the next general election, has retained his seat in parliament. His 'penalty' from the Parliamentary Commissioner for Standards, was to pay

back a fraction (£13,160) of the money that he used in this way.[21] In almost any other line of work, such behaviour could have led to legal proceedings for recovery. This highlighted a yawning gap between the standards to which MPs are held accountable and the sort of checks to which the majority of the working public are subject to. In response, a number of Conservative MPs wrote a joint letter to the *Telegraph* proposing the introduction of the recall:

> We recognise that we are accountable to our electorate and, consequently, we do not think that a parliamentary committee should have the discretion to expel an MP. However, we do think that consideration should be given to creating a recall mechanism, similar to that used in some US states, to enable constituents to vote on whether they remove their MP during the course of a parliament… a mechanism of this sort used in exceptional circumstances would increase MPs' accountability, address some of the frustration felt by a disenchanted public and help restore trust in our democratic institutions.[22]

In essence, such a scheme would permit citizens to petition to have their MP recalled from parliament and face a by-election in their constituency. The incumbent MP might still choose to stand but would need to fight to retain their seat all over again. This could at least prevent MPs like Derek Conway remaining in office after being discredited. However, there are problems with such an idea. Recall petitions could be used in marginal seats to re-fight general election results, which would undermine the mandate currently ensured by ordinary elections. They could be used tactically to distract MPs from parliamentary business. By-elections are also prohibitively expensive: the recent by-election to re-elect David Davis in Haltemprice and Howden was estimated to cost the taxpayer £200,000.[23]

To address these problems, some limitations would need to be placed on the recall. They should have a large petition requirement (15-20 per cent of registered voters in an MP's constituency). To prevent repeated elections, a recall attempt should only be permitted once during an MP's ordinary term of office. An alternative control would require an MP to be censured by the Parliamentary Commission for Standards before they were eligible to be recalled by their constituents. Recalls would not be commonly used under such a scheme but the mere fact that they could be activated by a dissatisfied electorate may alter the behaviour of MPs and may even encourage different sorts of people to stand for parliament. Given some limitations, the recall could offer parliament a valuable and publicly engaging accountability mechanism.

Term-limits

Introducing term-limits for MPs, and preventing them from standing for re-election after a set number of terms in office would mark a radical change in the composition of parliament. The central question of whether this would benefit policymaking and legislation is difficult to answer at this stage; especially since legislative term-limits are a recent phenomenon in US states. However, there are some distinct advantages to introducing them. Suppose, for example, that MPs would have to give up their seat after holding two or three terms in parliament (or 10 or 15 years). The results would be as follows:

- A faster turnover of MPs would increase the number of people that have a chance to take up seats in parliament at some point during their lives.

- Political careers would be shorter, making more seats available to those who are unable or unwilling to devote their entire life to politics. This might help, in particular, to address the lack of representation of women and minority groups in parliament, and encourage those with experience outside of politics to stand for parliament.

- The advantage to incumbent MPs at general elections would be time-limited.

- Career politicians would find it more difficult to gain permanent 'footholds' in the political system, reducing the number of people who become permanently dependent financially, and in terms of status, on holding political power.

There are some clear disadvantages as well. Term-limits go against the principle of the electorate being given the ultimate choice of who to elect to parliament; it would be arbitrary and unfair to deprive a particular constituency of a popular representative on the grounds that they had already served their maximum allotted time. In addition, parliament would lack more experienced members, who could steer legislation more effectively and offer greater expertise as ministers. However, while there is doubtless plenty of talent within parliament, the present system is arguably not especially adapted to using it effectively. MPs do not often appear to be selected to lead a department or take a position in the Cabinet due to their knowledge of a particular sector of government, and are more likely to be selected on the basis of an apparent pecking order, where what are perceived as the more important roles are handed to key players within the governing party. In light of this, it is sensible to contend that term-limits would represent an improvement on the current situation.

4. Citizen justice

A grand jury to investigate public officials
Another approach towards increasing the account-ability of public officials, and politicians in particular, would be to tighten up the current institutions of judicial oversight. The Labour government has intro-duced a number of laws to regulate the funding of political parties and campaigns under the Political Parties, Elections and Referendums Act 2000.[24] The intentions behind the legislation are laudable: to prevent secret donors from influencing policy and currying favour with those in high office, and to enforce far greater transparency than has ever been seen in British parliamentary democracy before.

Recent events, besides the already mentioned Derek Conway affair, however, suggest that there is a weakness in the enforcement of the laws that impact on MPs. First there was the 'cash-for-honours' scandal, implicating then Prime Minister Tony Blair and his aides, where a large number of secret loans to the Labour party turned out to correlate remarkably closely with the creditors receiving peerages.[25] Then there was a series of problems related to improperly or undeclared donations to the Labour party,[26] and Peter Hain's[27] and Harriet Harman's[28] campaigns for the deputy leadership, as well as Wendy Alexander's leadership campaign in Scotland.[29] All these cases have a common feature: none have led to prosecutions (although police investigations into Peter Hain's dealings are still open as of writing). In some of these cases, this might be due to a genuine lack of evidence, but in other instances, there is no doubt that rules have been broken, and that this has been in some cases admitted by the guilty party. There was no doubt that Wendy Alexander, for example, had failed to declare donations, as well as accepting a donation from a non UK-registered voter, but prosecutors found that bringing formal charges was 'not in the public interest'.[30]

This course of events does not seem consistent with the general understanding of how the criminal justice system is meant to work. It would be considered a bit strange if, having been caught red-handed committing a criminal offence such as theft or fraud, an ordinary citizen were able to admit to have broken 'the rules' (i.e. the law), and then expect not to face criminal proceedings. It is possible for citizens to come to an informal understanding, sometimes involving compensation to the victim, in which criminal charges prove unnecessary, but it is not clear anything equivalent to that has happened in these cases. The victims of the non-disclosure of donations are undoubtedly the electorate as a whole who, under the laws (with criminal penalties) that the government itself introduced, have a right to know how parties and campaigns are being funded. It is not clear how public prosecutors can establish on the public's behalf that it has been suitably compensated by, for example, a handful of resignations. Would an employer be content merely to have an employee who had been caught stealing resign their position but not face any criminal charges? It seems unlikely, and though the harm in this instance is far more dispersed amongst the general public, that does not make it any less real. When politicians appear almost impervious to prosecution, it stokes up public feeling that the law applies differently to officials. It is arguably a major source of damage to our political culture and makes people far more suspicious of democratic institutions, leading to more disengagement and apathy amongst the electorate.

So what is the solution? The decision over whether to proceed with a prosecution in the political arena needs to be removed from the institutions that are overseen by politicians. In other words, for the state to be held accountable to the law, the law must be exercised by an agency that is separate from the state, an agency that represents more directly the general public. We already have such an institution, the jury, for deciding whether an individual is innocent or guilty once they have been brought to trial, but public officials can avoid even reaching that stage at the moment. This institution could be expanded. Rather than having only government-employed public prosecutors to decide when public officials should be prosecuted, another route for those with evidence to prosecute public officials could be created. A grand jury of randomly selected citizens could be convened to investigate criminal activity within governing institutions and make the decision over whether to prosecute. Their decision would be based on their own independent deliberations of whether there was a case to answer and whether a prosecution was, *in their opinion only*, in the interest of the public, rather than any test set down in policy.

Using the federal grand jury in the US as a model, the jury would be made up of between 16 and 23 jurors and would elect a foreperson to lead the proceedings. Their deliberations would be held in private, with the identities of the jury kept secret until long after their term is complete. Besides having power to issue charges, they should have powers of investigation, to call witnesses to be interviewed and to call for documents to be brought for examination. They could also be given the power to issue search warrants. Although, in many cases, the police or the Electoral Commission would approach the jury to request a prosecution, a key feature of their openness would be that anyone could bring charges before them and offer evidence to persuade them. It would be prudent to have an assistant with knowledge of the law available to be consulted, but not to direct the jury as a judge can in ordinary criminal trials. It would also be useful for juries to be given an estimate of what mounting each prosecution will cost the public.

This would be another radical change to the level of scrutiny that citizens have over public officials, but something of this nature is required in order to ensure that no set of people, no matter how influential, are able to act above the law.

Citizen prosecutors

Vulnerabilities in the criminal justice system are not limited to its ability to deal with public officials. A recent Civitas report examines how central government targets have compromised the effectiveness of the police.[31] At the same time, sentencing decisions and the length of sentences for convicted criminals have to be rationed according to the number of prison places made available by the Home Office. The Crown Prosecution Service, the United Kingdom's public prosecutor represents another major weakness. As is often the case with any large centralised organisation, the CPS suffers from tremendous inefficiencies and poor performance. Because of this, as documented in some detail by both the National Audit Office[32] and its own inspectorate,[33] the CPS is frequently the weakest link when bringing criminal cases to a satisfactory conclusion. It frequently loses or mishandles important files which leads to failed trials and wasted time in court. If ever there were a candidate for increased local accountability where Whitehall and ministerial oversight has failed, the CPS is certainly a strong one.

In addition to this practical problem, there is also a point of principle about which body should decide whom and when to prosecute. Should it be a bureaucratic institution accountable to the political establishment, or the citizens themselves? In other words, could grand juries decide what is in the public interest better than the CPS? This is an open question in need of greater analysis, especially as the grand jury remains a controversial institution in many of the areas in which it is used in the US. As has been suggested above, the emphasis should be on permitting local experimentation within a broad framework. For example, local councils that felt their community was not well served by the CPS should be permitted as part of their home-rule powers to introduce a grand jury system for prosecuting individuals for crime committed in their districts. Introducing such an option would not be as difficult in the UK as elsewhere as there already exist the institutions necessary for convening ordinary juries to test serious criminal cases. Indeed, the grand jury is the one direct democratic institution that might be said to be 'native' to Britain.

Conclusion

Why would a more direct democracy be good for Britain? Many reasons are repeated so trivially that they are more like mantras than policies: listening to the people, citizens making their own laws and participating in policymaking, locally accountable officials and local priorities. It takes a devout contrarian in the present political climate to come out explicitly in favour of more power to central government, to politicians, bureaucrats and unelected officials, even if in many respects this is the actual direction of policy.

Beneath the rhetoric and the platitudes, however, there is a growing murmur for real reform of our political system. The notion of individuals possessing rights that need protection from the state is not peculiar to Britain but it has often been welcome here. From George Orwell's *Animal Farm* and *1984* to Douglas Adams' *Hitchhikers Guide to the Galaxy*, both our intellectual and popular culture has been imbued with a sometimes cheeky, often morbid, scepticism of the benefits of powerful government. This culture is expressed evenly on the left and the right of our nominal political spectrum and almost equally amongst political parties. It means that, although this report has undeniably approached the theme from a specifically classical liberal perspective, the importance of limiting the powers of representative government commands much more widespread support. Direct democracy is simply a tried-and-tested method of augmenting those checks and balances on government power.

The difficulty with suggesting any constitutional reform is that a person's support for it will tend to be predicated on their relationship to the current political establishment and to their support amongst the people. A political party might find itself championing the use of referendums when it agrees with opinion polls or electoral reform while in opposition, but find itself upholding 'principles' of parliamentary sovereignty once in power, even if they are articulated in order to justify a constitutional change.

That sort of self-interest will always play a role but it is not an overriding factor. Even if it were, political parties have enough hubris to introduce reforms that can later be turned against them. The Labour government introduced devolution to Scotland, gaining much popularity in the process and a new assembly that they controlled for many years. Yet that assembly also became a point of access for the Scottish National Party, a powerful competitor to Labour incumbents in both Scottish parliamentary and British parliamentary seats. Similarly, Labour introduced substantial new legislation relating to political donations in a coup that helped to demonstrate Labour's commitment to clean politics against the Conservatives' reputation for sleaze. They impaled themselves on this spiky legislation years later having failed to follow their own laws when party finances tightened. The beneficiaries of these radical reforms are certainly not the Labour Party itself and are arguably, in each case, to the advantage of the electorate as a whole. This shows it is certainly possible for our democratic system to reform positively, even if in other ways it has come perilously close to permanently diminishing itself.

Final words of caution are simply 'accept no substitutes'. Policies given a direct-democratic spin can still fail to give more powers to citizens if they do not include statutory powers to reject the wishes and beliefs of public officials and offer alternatives directly to the people. Those powers, whether legislating or judicial, are the key ingredient to any reform, and any reform lacking them is likely to be without substance.

Notes

1. What is Direct Democracy?

1   Ancient History Sourcebook: Thucydides (c.460/455-c.399 BCE): Pericles' Funeral Oration from the *Peloponnesian War* (Book 2.34-46); http://www.fordham.edu/halsall/ancient/pericles-funeralspeech.html

2   Hague, R. and Harrop M., 'Democracy', in *Comparative Government and Politics: an introduction*, 6th edn, Palgrave Macmillan, 2004.

3   House of Commons Information Office: 'You and Your MP', Factsheet M1, Members Series, March 2008: http://www.parliament.uk/documents/upload/m01.pdf

4   See the description of the Athenian judicial system in Blackwell, C., *Demos: Classical Athenian Democracy, A publication of The Stoa*, March 2003: http://www.stoa.org/projects/demos/article_intro_legal_syste m?page=1&greekEncoding=

5   BBC news: 'School leaving age plans unveiled', 6 November 2007: http://news.bbc.co.uk/1/hi/education/7080699.stm

6   Wintour, P., 'Labour forum backs voting age 16', *Guardian*, 28 July 2008: http://www.guardian.co.uk/politics/2008/jul/28/labour.lords

7   Rousseau, J., *The Social Contract (1762)*, Book Three, Section 15, translated in *Social Contract: Essays by Locke, Hume, Rousseau*, London: OUP, 1971, p. 260.

8   Barker, E. (1948), *Social Contract: Essays by Locke, Hume, Rousseau*, p. xxxiv.

9   Barker, E. (1948), *Social Contract: Essays by Locke, Hume, Rousseau*, p. xxxiv.

10   Rousseau, J., *The Social Contract translated in Social Contract: Essays by Locke, Hume, Rousseau*, p. 260.

11   See, for example, the Heritage Foundation's Index of Economic Freedom:
     http://www.heritage.org/Index/topten.cfm
     and Reporters Without Border's ranking of press freedom:
     http://www.rsf.org/article.php3?id_article=24025

12   Beedham, B., 'Power to the people: the case for Direct Democracy', in *Civitas Review* Vol. 3, Issue 2, Civitas, June 2006: http://civitas.org.uk/pdf/CivitasReviewJune06.pdf

13   See Lund, N., *Rousseau and Direct Democracy (with a Note on the Supreme Court's Term-limits Decision)*, George Mason Law & Economics Research Paper No. 03-41, 2003-2004:
     http://papers.ssrn.com/sol3/papers.cfm?abstract_id=442061

2: The American Way

1   I&R Historical Timeline, Initiative and Referendum Institute:
     http://www.iandrinstitute.org/New%20IRI%20Website%20In
     fo/Drop%20Down%20Boxes/Quick%20Facts/Almanac%20-
     %20I&R%20Historical%20Timeline.pdf

2   I&R Historical Timeline, Initiative and Referendum Institute:
     http://www.iandrinstitute.org/New%20IRI%20Website%20In
     fo/Drop%20Down%20Boxes/Quick%20Facts/Almanac%20-
     %20I&R%20Historical%20Timeline.pdf

3   States with Legislative Referendum (LR) for Statutes and Constitutional Amendments, Initiative and Referendum Institute:
     http://www.iandrinstitute.org/New%20IRI%20Website%20In

fo/Drop%20Down%20Boxes/Requirements/Legislative%20R
eferendum%20States.pdf

4   'Constitutional Amendments', Report 2006-03, Initiative and
    Referendum Institute, October 2006:
    http://www.iandrinstitute.org/REPORT%202006-
    3%20Amendments.pdf

5   Tolbert, C., 'Direct Democracy as a catalyst for 21st Century
    Political Reform', Kent State University, Ohio, p. 10:
    http://www.iandrinstitute.org/New%20IRI%20Website%20In
    fo/I&R%20Research%20and%20History/I&R%20Studies/
    Tolbert%20%20DD%20as%2021st%20Century%20Reform%2
    0Catalyst%20IRI.pdf

6   Tolbert, C., 'Direct Democracy as a catalyst for 21st Century
    Political Reform', Kent State University, Ohio, p. 10.

7   Haskell, J., *Direct Democracy or Representative Government?*,
    Boulder, Colorado: Westview Press, 2001, p. 65.

8   Braunstein, R., *Initiative and Referendum Voting*, New York:
    LFB Scholarly Publishing LLC, 2004, p. 16.

9   Braunstein, *Initiative and Referendum Voting*, 2004, p. 17.

10 I&R Historical Timeline, Initiative and Referendum Institute,
    p. 16.

11 I&R Historical Timeline, Initiative and Referendum Institute,
    p. 16.

12 Tolbert, 'Direct Democracy as a catalyst for 21st Century
    Political Reform'.

13 Tolbert, 'Direct Democracy as a catalyst for 21st Century
    Political Reform'.

14 Statewide Initiatives Since 1904-2000, Initiative and
   Referendum Institute:
   http://www.iandrinstitute.org/New%20IRI%20Website%20In
   fo/Drop%20Down%20Boxes/Historical/Statewide
   %20Initiatives%201904-2000.pdf

15 Tolbert, 'Direct Democracy as a catalyst for 21st Century
   Political Reform'.

16 Spivak, J., 'Why Did California Adopt the Recall?', History
   News Network, 15 September 2003:
   http://hnn.us/articles/1682.html

17 Cronin, T., *Direct Democracy: The politics of Initiative,
   Referendum and Recall*, Cambridge, Massachusetts: Harvard
   University Press, 1999, p. 126.

18 Haskell, *Direct Democracy or Representative Government?*,
   2001, p. 53.

19 Matsusaka, J., 'Direct Democracy and Public Employees',
   University of Southern California, May 2007:
   http://www.iandrinstitute.org/Symposium2007/
   Matsusaka.pdf

20 'Overview of Initiative Use 1904-2006', Initiative and
   Referendum Institute, November 2006:
   http://www.iandrinstitute.org/IRI%20Initiative%20
   Use%20(2006-11).pdf

21 Moore, S., 'Proposition 13 Then, Now and Forever', Cato
   Institute, Washington D.C., July 1996:
   http://www.cato.org/pub_display.php?pub_id=5682

22 'Overview of Initiative Use 1904-2006', Initiative and
   Referendum Institute, November 2006:

http://www.iandrinstitute.org/IRI%20Initiative%20Use%20(2
006-11).pdf;
'Election 2008: A first look at results', Initiative and
Referendum Institute, November 2008:
http://www.iandrinstitute.org/BW%202008-
3%20Results%20v2.pdf

23 Haskell, *Direct Democracy or Representative Government?*,
    2001, p. 65.

24 Lapriore, E., 'Few Can Speak for Many in US Politics',
    University of Southern California News, California, April 2004:
    http://www.usc.edu/uscnews/stories/10614.html

25 Piper, B., 'A Brief Analysis of Voter Behaviour Regarding
    Tax Initiative', *Initiative & Referendum Institute*, 2001:
    http://www.iandrinstitute.org/New%20IRI%20Website%20In
    fo/I&R%20Research%20and%20History/I&R%20Studies/Pipe
    r%20-%20I&R%20Tax%20Measures%201978%20-
    %201999%20IRI.pdf

26 Piper, 'A Brief Analysis of Voter Behaviour Regarding Tax
    Initiative', *Initiative & Referendum Institute*, 2001.

27 Piper, 'A Brief Analysis of Voter Behaviour Regarding Tax
    Initiative', *Initiative & Referendum Institute*, 2001.

28 Lapriore, 'Few Can Speak for Many in US Politics', *University
    of Southern California News*, 2004.

29 Matsusaka, J., 'Direct Democracy and Public Employees',
    University of Southern California, May 2008 (this is an update
    of the paper of the same name cited above but is not yet
    available online)

30 Matsusaka, 'Direct Democracy and Public Employees',
    University of Southern California, 2008.

31 Matsusaka, 'Direct Democracy and Public Employees', *University of Southern California*, 2008.

32 Statewide Initiatives Since 1904-2000, Initiative and Referendum Institute.

33 'Ballotwatch: Election Results 2006', Initiative and Referendum Institute, November 2006: http://www.iandrinstitute.org/BW%202006-5%20(Election%20results).pdf

34 For an overview see: Kelo v. New London, PBS, June 2005: http://www.pbs.org/now/politics/domaindebate.html

35 'Ballotwatch: Election Results 2006', Initiative and Referendum Institute, November 2006.

3: The Mechanisms of Direct Democracy

1 Signature, Geographic Distribution and Single Subject (SS) Requirements for Initiative Petitions, Initiative and Referendum Institute: http://www.iandrinstitute.org/New%20IRI%20Website%20Info/Drop%20Down%20Boxes/Requirements/Almanac%20-%20Signature%20and%20SS%20and%20GD%20Requirements.pdf

2 Signature, Geographic Distribution and Single Subject (SS) Requirements for Initiative Petitions, Initiative and Referendum Institute: http://www.iandrinstitute.org/New%20IRI%20Website%20Info/Drop%20Down%20Boxes/Requirements/Almanac%20-%20Signature%20and%20SS%20and%20GD%20Requirements.pdf

3 'Constitutional Amendments', Report 2006-03, Initiative and Referendum Institute, October 2006:

http://www.iandrinstitute.org/REPORT%202006-3%20Amendments.pdf

4   States with Legislative Referendum (LR) for Statutes and Constitutional Amendments, Initiative and Referendum Institute: http://www.iandrinstitute.org/New%20IRI%20Website%20Info/Drop%20Down%20Boxes/Requirements/Legislative%20Referendum%20States.pdf

5   'What are ballot propositions, initiatives and referendums?', Initiative and Referendum Institute: http://www.iandrinstitute.org/Quick%20Fact%20-%20What%20is%20I&R.htm

6   See the Colorado State Constitution: http://www.i2i.org/Publications/ColoradoConstitution/cnart5.htm

7   Comparisons of Statewide Initiative Processes, Initiative and Referendum Institute: http://www.iandrinstitute.org/New%20IRI%20Website%20Info/Drop%20Down%20Boxes/Requirements/A%20Comparison%20of%20Statewide%20I&R%20Processes.pdf

8   Comparisons of Statewide Initiative Processes, Initiative and Referendum Institute: http://www.iandrinstitute.org/New%20IRI%20Website%20Info/Drop%20Down%20Boxes/Requirements/A%20Comparison%20of%20Statewide%20I&R%20Processes.pdf

9   Signature, Geographic Distribution and Single Subject (SS) Requirements for Initiative Petitions, Initiative and Referendum Institute: http://www.iandrinstitute.org/New%20IRI%20Website%20Info/Drop%20Down%20Boxes/Requirements/Almanac%20-

%20Signature%20and%20SS%20and%20GD%20Requirement
s.pdf

10 See Text of Proposition 22, *California Secretary of State*:
http://primary2000.sos.ca.gov/VoterGuide/Propositions/22te
xt.htm

11 'California Supreme Court Rules in Marriage Cases', Judicial
Council of California, 15 May 2008:
http://www.courtinfo.ca.gov/presscenter/newsreleases/NR26
-08.PDF

12 See Text of Proposition 8, *California Secretary of State*:
http://www.sos.ca.gov/elections/bp_11042008_pres_general/
prop_8_titlesummary.pdf

13 'Election 2008: A first look at results', Initiative and
Referendum Institute, November 2008:
http://www.iandrinstitute.org/BW%202008-
3%20Results%20v2.pdf

14 For a civil liberty orientated overview, see Harper, J., 'The
REAL ID Act: An Update', Washington DC: Cato Institute, 8
October 2007: http://www.cato.org/tech/tk/071008-tk.html

15 See the exchange as described by pressure group,
DownsizeDC:
http://www.downsizedc.org/blog/chertoff_threatens_govern
or_governor_threatens_chertoff

16 Figures based on *Rule in America: A Fifty-State Handbook.*
Congressional Quarterly Press, 2001, cited by the South
Carolina Civic Education Project:
http://www.cas.sc.edu/poli/civiced/Reference%20Materials/
US_home_rule.htm

17 'Recall of State Officials', *National Conference of State Legislatures*, March 2006:
http://www.ncsl.org/programs/legismgt/elect/recallprovision.htm

18 'Recall of Local Officials', *National Conference of State Legislatures*, 2006:
http://www.ncsl.org/programs/legismgt/elect/localrecall.htm

19 'Recall of State Officials', *National Conference of State Legislatures*, 2006.

20 'Recall of State Officials', *National Conference of State Legislatures*, 2006.

21 Cronin, T., *Direct Democracy: The politics of Initiative, Referendum and Recall*, Cambridge, Massachusetts: Harvard University Press, 1999, p. 127.

22 Lund, N., *Rousseau and Direct Democracy (with a Note on the Supreme Court's Term-limits Decision)*, George Mason Law & Economics Research Paper No. 03-41, 2003-2004:
http://papers.ssrn.com/sol3/papers.cfm?abstract_id=442061

23 See US Term-limits website:
http://www.termlimits.org/content.asp?pl=18&sl=19&contentid=19

24 See *The Book of the States, 2007*, Council of State Government, p. 197, cited by the National Governor's Association:
http://www.nga.org/files/pdf/BOS4-9.pdf

25 Brenner, S., 'The Voice of the Community: A case for Grand Jury Independence', *Virginia Journal of Social Policy & The Law*, 1995:
http://campus.udayton.edu/~grandjur/recent/lawrev.htm

26 Edwards, G., *The Grand Jury*, Philadelphia: Law Booksellers, 1906: http://www.constitution.org/gje/gj_00.htm

27 Brenner, S., 'Federal Grand Juries', University of Dayton School of Law: http://campus.udayton.edu/~grandjur/fedj/fedj.htm

28 Brenner, 'The Voice of the Community: A case for Grand Jury Independence', 1995: http://campus.udayton.edu/~grandjur/recent/lawrev.htm

29 Dillard, W., Johnson S. and Lynch, T., 'A Grand Façade: How the Grand Jury Was Captured by Government', Washington DC, Cato Institute, 2003: http://www.cato.org/pubs/pas/html/pa476/pa476index.html

30 Rosenzweig, P., 'Time Is Now For Federal Grand Jury Reform', Washington DC: Heritage Foundation, 21 February 2003: http://www.heritage.org/Press/Commentary/ed022103a.cfm

31 Brenner, S., 'Power to Abolish the Grand Jury', University of Dayton School of Law: http://campus.udayton.edu/~grandjur/stategj/abolish.htm

32 Karson, L., 'The Implications of a Key-Man System for Selecting a Grand Jury: An Exploratory Study', *Southwest Journal of Criminal Justice*, vol. 3(1), 2006, pp. 3-16: http://swjcj.cjcenter.org/archives/3.1/Karson.pdf

33 Karson, 'The Implications of a Key-Man System for Selecting a Grand Jury: An Exploratory Study', *Southwest Journal of Criminal Justice*, 2006, pp. 3-16.

4: Why the UK Needs Democratic Reform

1   http://www.epolitix.com/EN/Interviews/200801/f524ad79-355a-46f7-ae42-3bbecdca2754.htm

2   Legislative and Regulatory Reform Bill, Session 2005-06,
    House of Commons:
    http://www.publications.parliament.uk/pa/cm200506/cmbills
    /111/06111.1-4.html

3   Howarth, D., 'Who wants the Abolition of Parliament Bill?',
    The Times, February 21 2006:
    http://www.timesonline.co.uk/tol/comment/columnists/gues
    t_contributors/article733022.ece

4   Spencer, J.R., *et al.*, 'Legislative Reform', Letters, *The Times*,
    16 February 2006:
    http://www.timesonline.co.uk/tol/comment/letters/article731
    111.ece

5   Spencer, *et al.*, 'Legislative Reform', Letters, *The Times*, 16
    February 2006.

6   Parliamentary Brief: 'Legislative and Regulatory Reform
    Bill', *Law Society*, 9 February 2006:
    http://www.lawsociety.org.uk/secure/file/152472/e:/teamsite-
    deployed/documents/templatedata/Internet%20Documents/
    Parliamentary%20briefings/Documents/legregrefbillhoc2ndr
    eading090206.pdf

7   Parliamentary Brief: 'Legislative and Regulatory Reform
    Bill', *Law Society*, 9 February 2006.

8   'Lords Critical over Government over Handling of
    Legislative and Regulatory Reform Bill', UK Parliament, 8
    June 2006:
    http://www.parliament.uk/parliamentary_committees/lords_
    press_notices/pn080606const.cfm

9   'Lords Critical over Government over Handling of
    Legislative and Regulatory Reform Bill', UK Parliament, 8
    June 2006.

10 'The Government's approach to legislation with constitutional issues' in the Eleventh report of the House of Lords Constitution Committee, Sessions 2005-06, 24 May 2006:
http://www.publications.parliament.uk/pa/ld200506/ldselect/ldconst/194/19404.htm

11 'The Government's approach to legislation with constitutional issues' in the Eleventh report of the House of Lords Constitution Committee, Sessions 2005-06, 24 May 2006.

12 Cracknell, R., 'Acts & Statutory Instruments: Volume of UK legislation 1950 to 2007', SN/SG/2911, House of Commons Library, 23 January 2008:
http://www.parliament.uk/commons/lib/research/notes/snsg-02911.pdf

13 *The Governance of Britain – Draft Constitutional Renewal Bill*, Ministry of Justice, March 2008:
http://www.justice.gov.uk/docs/draft-constitutional-renewal-bill.pdf

14 *First Report of the Joint Committee on the Draft Constitutional Renewal Bill*, 31 July 2008:
http://www.publications.parliament.uk/pa/jt200708/jtselect/jtconren/166/16611.htm#a133

15 'Less Regulation: 4 ways to cut the burden of EU red tape', *Open Europe*, November 2005:
http://www.openeurope.org.uk/research/regs.pdf

16 See 'A Guide to the Constitutional Treaty', 2nd edn, *Open Europe*, February 2008:
http://www.openeurope.org.uk/research/guide.pdf

17 Interview with Pierre Manent in *Le Point*, issue 1746, 17 January 2007: http://www.lepoint.fr/actualites-

chroniques/manent-liberal-patriote/989/0/27044 (translation
provided by:
http://galliawatch.blogspot.com/2007/12/reason-for-
nations.html)

5: Introducing Direct Democracy to the UK

1 Richards, S., 'Don't be fooled — these "heroic campaigns"
only make our democracy even more fragile', *Independent*, 17
June 2008:
http://www.independent.co.uk/opinion/commentators/steve
-richards/steve-richards-dont-be-fooled-ndash-these-heroic-
campaigns-only-make-our-democracy-even-more-fragile-
848514.html

2 Pannick, D., 'No government should award itself
unreviewable powers', *The Times*, 3 July 2008:
http://business.timesonline.co.uk/tol/business/law/columnist
s/article4256096.ece

3 'Supreme Court', Ministry of Justice:
http://www.justice.gov.uk/whatwedo/supremecourt.htm

4 'Appointment of the first chief executive of the Supreme
Court', Ministry of Justice, 18 January 2008:
http://www.justice.gov.uk/news/announcement180108a.htm

5 Kimber, R., 'General Election, 5th May 2005', Political Science
Resources, 11 March 2008:
http://www.psr.keele.ac.uk/area/uk/ge05/results.htm

6 'Introduction to e-petitions', *Number10.gov.uk*:
http://petitions.pm.gov.uk/about

7 'PM emails road pricing signatories', *Number10.gov.uk*, 20
February 2007:
http://www.number10.gov.uk/output/Page11050.asp

8   'e-petitions', Written Ministerial Statement, *Parliamentary Business & News*, 22 July 2008: http://www.commonsleader.gov.uk/output/Page2536.asp

9   'Giving Parliament back its teeth', *Conservatives*, 6 June 2007: http://www.conservatives.com/tile.do?def=news.story.page&obj_id=137003

10 'Communities in Control', *Communities and Local Government*, 9 July 2008: http://www.communities.gov.uk/documents/communities/pdf/886045.pdf

11 'Communities in Control', *Communities and Local Government*, 9 July 2008, p. iii.

12 Jenkins, S., 'Tax and Policy? You're lucky to have parking tickets and big bags', *Guardian*, 11 July 2008: http://www.guardian.co.uk/commentisfree/2008/jul/11/localgovernment.localgovernment

13 Kenny, M., 'The trouble with iPod democracy', Institute for Public Policy Research, 12 July 2008: http://www.ippr.org/articles/?id=3206

14 Leeke, M., Sear C. and Gay, O., *An Introduction to Devolution in the UK,* Parliament and Constitute Centre, Research Paper 03/84 House of Commons Library, 17 November 2003, p. 3: http://www.parliament.uk/commons/lib/research/rp2003/rp03-084.pdf

15 Johnson, S., 'Alex Salmond demands preparation for Scottish independence begin', *Telegraph*, 29 July 2008: http://www.telegraph.co.uk/news/newstopics/politics/scotland/2463463/Alex-Salmond-demands-preparation-for-Scottish-independence-begin.html

16 McLean, I., Lodge, G. and Schmuecker, K., *Fair Shares? Barnett and the Politics of Public Expenditure*, Institute for Public Policy Research, 10 July 2008: http://www.ippr.org/publicationsandreports/publication.asp?id=619

17 Lettice, J., 'Scottish Parliament lines up against ID cards', Register, 25 February 2005: http://www.theregister.co.uk/2005/02/25/msps_oppose_id_scheme/

18 See de Waal, A., 'Fast Track to Slow Progress', Civitas, 5 August 2008: http://www.civitas.org.uk/pdf/FastTracktoSlowProgress.pdf

19 Children, Schools and Families Committee: *Testing and Assessment*, Third Report of Session 2007-08, House of Commons, 7 May 2008: http://www.publications.parliament.uk/pa/cm200708/cmselect/cmchilsch/169/169.pdf

20 Pearce, N., 'Oui, monsieur le ministre', Institute for Public Policy Research, 20 April 2007: http://www.ippr.org/articles/index.asp?id=2662

21 Swaine, J., 'Disgraced Tory MP Derek Conway given year to repay money', *Telegraph*, 28 July 2008: http://www.telegraph.co.uk/news/newstopics/politics/conservative/2464436/Disgraced-Tory-MP-Derek-Conway-given-year-to-repay-money.html

22 Gauke, D., *et al.*, 'Sanctions against MPs', Letters to the editor, *Telegraph*, 29 February 2008: http://www.telegraph.co.uk/opinion/main.jhtml?xml=/opinion/2008/02/29/nosplit/dt2901.xml#head2

23 Kirkup, J., 'David Davis by-election "will cost taxpayers £200,000"', *Telegraph*, 9 July 2008: http://www.telegraph.co.uk/news/newstopics/politics/22741 24/David-Davis-by-election-'will-cost-taxpayers-andpound200,000'.html

24 Political Parties, Elections and Referendums Act 2000, Office of Public Sector Information: http://www.opsi.gov.uk/ Acts/acts2000/ukpga_20000041_en_1

25 'Q&A: Cash-for-honours', *BBC news*, 20 July 2007: http://news.bbc.co.uk/1/hi/uk_politics/4812822.stm

26 'Q&A: Donations row legal implications', *BBC news*, 30 November 2007: http://news.bbc.co.uk/1/hi/uk_politics/7121013.stm

27 'Q&A: Hain's resignation', *BBC news*, 24 January 2008: http://news.bbc.co.uk/1/hi/uk_politics/7187458.stm

28 'Harman defends Abrahams Donation', *BBC news*, 27 November 2007: http://news.bbc.co.uk/1/hi/uk_politics/7115016.stm

29 'Q&A: Wendy Alexander donations row', *BBC news*, 28 June 2008: http://news.bbc.co.uk/1/hi/scotland/7479025.stm

30 'Alexander will not be prosecuted', *BBC news*: http://news.bbc.co.uk/1/hi/scotland/7281820.stm

31 Sergeant, H., *The Public and the Police*, London: Civitas, May 2008.

32 Bourn, J., *Effective Use of Magistrates Courts Hearings*, National Audit Office, 10 February 2006: http://www.nao.org.uk/publications/nao_reports/05-06/0506798.pdf

33 *File Management and Organisation*, HM Crown Prosecution Service Inspectorate, May 2008:
http://www.hmcpsi.gov.uk/reports/FEN_thm_report.pdf